W9-BXM-858

# PRAISE FOR *WHEN A CHILD DIES*

"What I find so helpful about *When a Child Dies* is that Claire not only shares her son and her family with us on a deep emotional level, but she also answers multiple questions we all have in a caring yet practical way. Her book brings comfort where there seems to be no comfort, and hope where there seems to be no hope. She has opened her heart to share her grace, learning, and wisdom as well as her pain. I am grateful to have read this."

—Jan Warner, author of *Grief Day by Day: Simple Practices and Daily Guidance for Living with Loss*

"The author skillfully explores the various ways a child's death impacts all aspects of one's life, including relationships, anger at God, and how friends and family can help. Claire's words are inspiring and hopeful, offering compassionate advice to grieving parents."

—Pamela D. Blair, PhD, psychotherapist and coauthor of *I Wasn't Ready to Say Goodbye*

"This book is a loving blend of the author's personal journey with the death of her son and supportive information that can help parents see light amidst the dark."

—Alan D. Wolfelt, PhD, CT, author, educator, and grief counselor

## PRAISE FROM BEREAVEMENT CLIENTS OF CLAIRE AAGAARD

"*When a Child Dies* is a gift to grieving families. The universal issues facing grieving families are addressed in a straightforward and experienced manner. As I read it, I was once again comforted by

Claire. She offers us hope, through love and compassion, that our child is not lost and forgotten."

—Dr. Deborah Cherry, Alex's mom

"There are no words to adequately express the true devastation when your child dies or how to navigate life in that devastation, but Claire's words come as close as any words can. It has been twelve years since my son Eric died. I didn't know how to help his sister and brother, his father, or his beloved girlfriend, but I had Claire. She helped all of us, and I am so very grateful."

—Eilene Okerblom, RN, Eric's mom

"As newly grieving parents, Claire became the tether barely holding my wife and me to the ground in the midst of a category five hurricane of sadness and despair. Knowing Claire had experienced what we had was the only thing that made her words have weight and meaning for us. My one wish after the unexpected death of my nine-year-old daughter was that no one else would ever have to experience that kind of loss. Knowing that is unfortunately not possible, having a book like Claire's is absolutely necessary for survival. Thank you, Claire!"

—James Friedrich, Aitana's dad

"We lost our beautiful grown daughter and were left in an awkward space with friends and family who wanted to comfort us but lacked the words. In reading Claire Aagaard's book, I found understanding, wisdom, encouragement, and the hope I needed to slowly begin to move forward again. Saying goodbye to our sweet Danielle will never be okay, but I feel hope for myself and our family as we learn how to navigate life without her."

—Debbie S. Jamison, Danielle's mom

"Claire is a gentle and soft wind that comes to people who have experienced the deepest grief just at the right time. She tells a story about how to be the strength of that wind to clean up the debris left behind from tragedy and still be a woman that can love more deeply and more profoundly."

—Syndi Ecker, MA, Amy's mom

"'Pain is pain is pain.' I read those words through tear-blurred eyes even fourteen years after the fact. We all enter this unwanted and wholly undeserved 'club' in our own unique way, yet Claire reminds us that we are not alone on this path and that our emotions, however torn and tattered, are justified, natural, and shared by far too many others."

—Stu Stoddard, Cy's dad

## PRAISE FROM GRIEF AND HEALTHCARE PROFESSIONALS

"Claire offers calm hope and gentle, unshakable assurance as she moves her clients through the survival of the days, months, and years they cannot imagine living through. She has woven a tapestry of warmth, love, comfort, and the grounding strength of experience that helps alleviate suffering and leads us all to a place of healing."

—Dianne Thompson, MA, hospice bereavement counselor

"Losing a child can feel as though you've been shoved into an inferno. Claire helps dress the wounds from a place of personal courage, helping to heal one's scars. Her wisdom offers hope and tools for transforming a broken heart into a glimmer of light."

—Jeffrey Friedman, MSW, PhD, grief counselor

"Because of Claire's personal experience with loss, the emotions she conveys allow her to connect with the bereaved while her many years as a bereavement counselor allow her to counsel with kindness and wisdom. When reading her book, I periodically felt Claire's caring reach through her written words as if she were in the room consoling me."

—Dr. David Palchak, MD

"*When a Child Dies* is beautifully written with clarity and compassion. It provides hope and guidance to parents feeling heartbroken, lost, and alone in their grief. This is a valuable and much needed resource for both parents and for the family members, friends, and professionals wanting to provide support to the bereaved."

—Pam Gillette, MS, LMFT

"There have been few books that I recommend over and over again. *When a Child Dies* is a slim volume, not because it doesn't contain useful information, but rather because it's not overloaded with fluff. This book will be of utmost value not only to parents who have lost a child, but also to all the friends, family members, and medical and mental health practitioners with whom those parents may interact."

—Dugald D. Chisholm, MD, child, adult, and family psychiatrist

"Claire was instrumental in founding a grief resource center that was so needed in our community. Over our lifetime, we sometimes meet individuals who inspire us to be more compassionate in our life journey—Claire Aagaard is such a person."

—Tina McEvoy, RN, BSN, former Director of Hospice Partners of the Central Coast in San Luis Obispo, CA

# WHEN A CHILD DIES

*A Hopeful Healing Guide for
Surviving the Loss of a Child*

claire aagaard

Copyright © 2022 by Claire Aagaard
Cover and internal design © 2022 by Sourcebooks
Cover design by Sourcebooks
Cover image © ipopba/Getty Images

Sourcebooks and the colophon are registered trademarks of Sourcebooks.

All rights reserved. No part of this book may be reproduced in any form or by
any electronic or mechanical means including information storage and retrieval
systems—except in the case of brief quotations embodied in critical articles or
reviews—without permission in writing from its publisher, Sourcebooks.

This publication is designed to provide accurate and authoritative information
in regard to the subject matter covered. It is sold with the understanding
that the publisher is not engaged in rendering legal, accounting, or other
professional service. If legal advice or other expert assistance is required,
the services of a competent professional person should be sought.—*From
a Declaration of Principles Jointly Adopted by a Committee of the American
Bar Association and a Committee of Publishers and Associations*

Published by Sourcebooks
P.O. Box 4410, Naperville, Illinois 60567-4410
(630) 961-3900
sourcebooks.com

Originally published in 2020 in the United States by Claire Aagaard.

Library of Congress Cataloging-in-Publication Data

Names: Aagaard, Claire, author.
Title: When a child dies : a hopeful healing guide for surviving the loss
  of a child / Claire Aagaard.
Description: Naperville, Illinois : Sourcebooks, [2022] | Includes index.
Identifiers: LCCN 2021052657 |
Subjects: LCSH: Parental grief. | Children--Death--Psychological aspects. |
  Bereavement.
Classification: LCC BF575.G7 A219 2022 | DDC 155.9/37085--dc23/eng/20211105
LC record available at https://lccn.loc.gov/2021052657

Printed and bound in the United States of America.
VP 10 9 8 7 6 5 4 3 2 1

Dedicated to our son
Eric William Aagaard and
all the children gone from
our lives too soon.

ERIC, AGE 19 MONTHS

ERIC AND CHRISTIAN,
1983, THREE WEEKS PRIOR
TO THE ACCIDENT

Family photo, November 2020

Photo credit: Amy Hinrichs Photography

# CONTENTS

# FOREWORD

The loss of a child completely unmoors you. Your stunned family is suddenly thrust into an unimaginable landscape with no signposts and no paths—just dark, jagged territory in all directions—that you are supposed to navigate, somehow. At the time, the chance of survival, let alone reaching a place where normal life is an option, seems minimal.

In our case, when we lost our son Justin over a decade ago, we found a Sherpa to guide us through. Her name is Claire Aagaard, and the book you are about to read is the distillation of her professional and personal life in this landscape of loss. It was extremely important to us that Claire had already done (and is still doing) this journey herself. Her knowledge is earned, her experience is felt, not abstract.

It is not an exaggeration to say that Claire saved our lives. We will never stop grieving, but we are living a fuller and more joyful life than we ever thought possible, thanks to her.

As a professional grief counselor, Claire helped many people like us by patiently, lovingly, honestly, and generously sharing her own journey as a way of easing ours. Now, she has put her guidance on paper to be used more widely. Our family and friends did not know how to help us, or even talk to us, when we lost our son. And we did not know what to tell them. This book will help, greatly.

I am deeply sorry if you need this book, but I'm glad you have it. Nothing really makes this journey easier, but not walking it alone makes it possible.

Tony Peckham

# INTRODUCTION

There is no footprint too small to
leave an imprint on the world.
UNKNOWN

In April of 1992, nearly seven years after the death of my son Eric, I answered an ad from a local hospice looking for volunteers to form a children's bereavement team. The goal of this task force would be to provide education, primarily within the school system, on the effects of death and grief for children. Because my older son, Christian, had been five years old when his brother died, I knew I had a story to share and some insights that could be helpful. Although hampered by pervasive feelings of low self-esteem—and frankly terrified—at entering this arena, I felt strongly motivated to make every effort possible to give Eric's life continued meaning and purpose.

Not long after joining as a volunteer, the executive director of the hospice offered me a job as the assistant volunteer coordinator. Working in the field of death and dying amongst compassionate and skilled mental health professionals was life altering for me. I was lovingly encouraged to tell my story, and with that came the recognition of how much unresolved grief I was carrying. The need to enter counseling in order to do this work was an obvious next step, and one I took. I could not have been given a greater gift at this achingly vulnerable time in my life.

My work in hospice evolved, and a few years later—after more education, training, and incredible mentoring—I found myself at a comprehensive hospice program as their bereavement coordinator. The program quickly grew and with it also came requests from the community to assist individuals dealing with the aftermath of a sudden death who were not part of the hospice program.

With my colleague Dianne Thompson, I took extensive critical incident training to address this need. These new skills gave us the opportunity to respond to local tragedies, including the 2003 earthquake in our community where two residents died and many more were traumatized by the tragic event. We were then prepared to travel to Louisiana and Mississippi to offer emotional support to those suffering in the wake of Hurricane Katrina in 2005.

In 2007, I became the director of the Center for Grief, Education, and Healing. It was at this time that I traveled several times to Fort Collins, Colorado, to study with Alan Wolfelt, PhD, to complete his Death and Life Studies Program in order to move forward in obtaining my certification as a grief counselor.

Together with Dianne Thompson, my cofounder of the Center, we offered professional grief counseling to hospice families and specialized in working with families who were coping with the trauma of an unexpected death.

During those twenty-plus years in the field, I was privileged to work with every type of loss imaginable, but I was frequently called upon to assist parents whose child had died. I dedicated every one of those cases to my sweet Eric and always felt it was a tangible way to honor his life.

After retiring from bereavement work in 2016, I knew in my heart I needed to eventually write a book about child loss.

My hope was that it could be handed to a newly grieving parent and provide them with information, advice, and comfort from the perspective of another bereaved parent and a professional counselor with valuable years of experience. I learned so much from every grieving family who courageously walked through the doors and generously shared the heartache of losing their child. Their wisdom was something I wanted to share with others walking that same path.

Families come in all sizes and shapes—from traditional family backgrounds to divorced or blended families, single-parent households, and those from the LGBTQ+ community. My own experiences come from a traditional family situation, and I write from that place. However, my belief is that the thread that connects us is stronger than our differences, and the feelings of loss, sadness, and despair we face after the loss of a child are universal. While doing this work with bereaved parents, it was always my deepest wish that no other parent would ever have to suffer the loss of their child, all the while knowing that wish could never come true.

Having said that, if you are a newly grieving parent starting this book, please accept my sincerest condolences for your devastating loss. It is my heartfelt hope that this book will be of help to you. I hope it will help you feel less alone and isolated and will serve as a guide as you navigate the difficult journey through your grief.

# MY STORY

i carry your heart with me /
(i carry it in my heart)

E. E. CUMMINGS

Every parent who has lost a child has a story to tell that is painful, raw, and deeply personal. I believe it's vitally important that every parent tell and retell their story as many times as they need to. In my work as a grief counselor, it was my profound honor to listen to each story, and I always felt so privileged to be trusted to hear and hold them with the reverence they deserved.

In sitting down to write this book, I quickly realized how important it would be to share my own story; to be honest and authentic in order to connect in a place of shared vulnerability with every grieving parent. I don't know how you feel, but I do know the pain of child loss and all the ways in which it affects every aspect of your life. I hope the sharing of my story helps you move through this book with that bond of shared support and understanding.

It was a typical November morning in Atascadero, California—sun shining but crisp and cold. My husband Jim was off to work, and I was busy trying to corral my sons, four-and-a-half-year-old Christian and twenty-month-old Eric. It was a Friday, so a preschool morning for Christian. Before I dropped him off, though, my plan was to drive over to my sister Cincy's house to get a workout in. She and her family lived about a mile and a half away on a thoroughbred horse farm they owned and managed. She often watched the boys for me early in the morning so I could get my run in before the rest of the day unfolded for both of us. I remember thinking I wouldn't go that morning but talked myself back into it with the mental reminder of how good I always felt afterward. In addition, I wanted to confer with Cincy regarding a baby shower we were hosting the next day for our sister Jani, who was expecting her first child.

Just before we left the house, there was a monumental moment as Eric urgently asked to sit on the potty—a first! Christian was watching, of course, and when Eric "produced," there were shouts of amazement, enthusiastic clapping, and hugs all around. Life was crazy and perfect.

After my run, Cincy and I chatted in her enclosed back porch as I prepared to leave. Her two youngest, aged ten and twelve, were home, and they headed outside with Christian following behind.

As Cincy and I discussed shower plans, Eric became antsy, asking to go out with the other kids. "No, baby," Cincy told him.

"It's OK," I assured her. "I'm heading out now, too."

Eric dashed out as I opened the door, and we started to follow when I remembered I'd left his jacket behind. I quickly went back into the adjoining kitchen and called to Cincy when I couldn't find it. She came in to show me where it was, and we headed back out, all the while assuming Eric was with the big kids playing on the lawn. At this point, two or three minutes had passed. Once outside we saw no one there, and unfazed, continued out to an open area where my car was parked, and called for the children. Cincy's kids and Christian appeared, without Eric. When asked where he was, they quickly replied they hadn't seen him and didn't know he had even come outside.

Every parent knows that sinking feeling when a child is missing, even briefly. Cincy and I looked at one another and, without a word, ran to their backyard pool. As it was late November and not being used, the pool was covered with a detachable, floating cover (subsequently outlawed). We lifted the end of it and heaved a sigh of relief when we saw no sign of Eric. That relief was short-lived though as we now realized all the other potential hazards present with horse paddocks all around and the accompanying equipment of a working farm.

A search party quickly ensued with my brother-in-law Wally and other farm employees joining in. As each minute passed, the feelings of panic and impending doom enveloped me. "Something bad has happened, I just feel it. Maybe someone drove in and took him," I said.

"Don't be ridiculous," Wally replied. "He's here somewhere. We'll find him."

Wally, Cincy, and I circled around the back of the house for the second time, and as we neared the pool, I saw two farm workers pulling my son out of the water. He was blue and lifeless. The men who found him quickly started CPR, and 9-1-1 was called.

I could never adequately describe the scene at that moment or my reactions and feelings.

I assumed my son was dead. And I wanted to be as

well. The only thing close to being as traumatic and hor-
rific as those few moments was telling my husband what
had happened when he drove in just after the paramedics.

Eric was transported to a local hospital where, after
what seemed to be an eternity (probably an hour), they
told us he was breathing on his own but was unrespon-
sive. I was terrified to see him after my last glimpse of him
poolside, but he looked angelic and peaceful, with just a
small bump on his head. As we stood there beside his bed,
I saw him do what is called "posturing," where his body
stiffened with palms turned outward and toes turned in.
From my days as an X-ray tech in the ER, I knew this to
be a sign of brain damage, and my heart sank.

A decision was made to airlift Eric to Stanford
Medical Center in Palo Alto. The team that flew down
to pick him up somberly warned us it was highly likely
Eric could die in transport and to be prepared. How do
you prepare for that? We had no idea.

We went home and hastily packed, being sure to
include "Monk," Eric's favorite stuffed monkey. Jani
handed us a cooler of food, and she and her husband
Jan stayed at the house with Christian until Jim's parents
arrived from Los Angeles, two hundred miles south of us.

On the three-and-a-half-hour drive to Palo Alto,
we talked about what we might be facing. We tried to

remember the procedures the physicians told us they were likely to perform on Eric, but foremost in our minds was the terrifying possibility he had died during the flight. When we reached the parking lot at Stanford, we hugged each other hard and attempted to steel ourselves for what lay ahead. Night had fallen, and we felt very much alone. Leaving our small town and entering a world-famous medical center felt overwhelming and intimidating. Would we be just another unfortunate family? Would they care about our precious son the way we needed and wanted them to? Our family, our pediatrician, our support system, and all we cared about felt so very far away.

As we exited the elevator and entered the pediatric ICU, we were greeted by an RN who knew our names and, with tears in her eyes, told us how sorry she was that our son had been so severely injured. She will never know how much her empathy and kind manner meant to us in that moment. Eric's physician then introduced himself and attempted to prepare us before we walked into the room to see him.

Medical staff had inserted a bolt into Eric's skull that measured the pressure in his brain due to swelling, a consequence of near-drowning cases. He was also on a ventilator now, as they had put him in an induced coma to allow the brain to rest. Additionally, he had an IV and oxygen monitor.

As we stood by his bed viewing all this equipment and all that had been "done" to him, all I could think to say was, "I use a warm washcloth to wipe his bottom because wipes are too cold." As a mom who tried to parent with gentleness and love, that physical assault on Eric's body, however necessary, felt horrifying and indescribable. We all stood in silence for a few minutes looking at this small, beautiful little boy. Somehow it felt reassuring that Jim and I weren't the only ones in the room crying.

Eric was in the highest level of the Stanford pediatric ICU for three weeks. This is no place anyone would ever want to find themselves. Every child in this room was in extremely critical condition, and changes happened so quickly it was terrifying to leave for any extended period of time. My heart always pounded as we re-entered the room after even a thirty- to forty-minute break, because, in that pre-cell phone age, you were never sure what may have happened in your absence. Three children died in those three weeks after Eric was admitted.

Eric's prognosis continued to be dire, and eventually, his team called a meeting to ask us to make some major decisions. After removing all the equipment and bringing him out of the induced coma, he had not improved.

He had no gag reflex, was unable to blink, and existed in what they named a "vegetative state." His brain was severely damaged with only a small portion of the brain stem functioning, telling him to breathe.

Did we want to have a feeding tube inserted in his stomach to prolong life? Did we want CPR performed if his heart stopped? His kind and loving physician—the father of two young sons himself—said no parent should ever have to be asked these questions, but he needed our answers.

Thankfully, Jim and I were in total agreement. Of course, we were willing to accept Eric in any way or form he came and would continue to love him with all our hearts. However, we would not be so selfish as to prolong his life in a vegetative state by artificial means just to have him with us. We opted to leave in his nasogastric tube for feeding and allow medications and treatments to ensure he did not suffer. The team all believed he would likely die in the next few days or weeks.

Eric was moved to a step-down unit and over the next couple of weeks made no improvement. We had another conference with our doctors and made the decision to move him across the street to Stanford Children's Hospital where every effort to "rehab" him would be made. We were told the longer he went without any sign of improvement, the less likely it would be that he would recover.

The children's hospital was overwhelming in every imaginable way. As you entered the lobby, dolls, pictures, and memorabilia donated by Shirley Temple filled glass cases and captured your attention. Many of the young patients were battling cancer, and as you walked down the long halls to your own child's room, you were likely to pass these children in wheelchairs or walking with their IV poles, bald and pale, yet animated and chatting with their parents or one another.

The other prevalent disease afflicting many there was cystic fibrosis, a pulmonary disease, which required a percussion of the chest to remove obstructive secretions. One of the strongest memories I have of the time spent at Children's is the sound of a physical therapist "clapping" a child's chest, the "thump, thump" resonating loudly as you walked down the hall.

Eric's condition remained unchanged, except for a bout of aspiration pneumonia, which we treated with antibiotics. Our decision to do so was based on our physician's belief the pneumonia could be resolved and would make him more comfortable. The mindset of "comfort care" for Eric became our compass and driving force as we navigated this unfamiliar territory.

Another conference was held, and somber medical staff now asked us where we wanted to "place" him. He was deemed too unstable to bring home, which was our desire, but not critical enough to remain in a hospital. We were told there were facilities (that word felt like a knife in my heart) in Fresno or Los Angeles, each two to three hours away, with the distance being only one of the many objections we had. I remembered a letter I had received from Sjany de Groot, an RN who had a small nursing home for children in San Luis Obispo, just twenty minutes from our home. She had read about Eric's accident in the local paper and offered to take him, should the need arise.

At the beginning of February 1984, approximately ten weeks after his near-drowning accident, we transferred Eric to the de Groot Nursing Home. It was a beautiful home, sunny and bright, filled with positive energy and loving care. Sjany and her husband were Dutch and spoke with thick accents.

It was home to about eight to ten other children at the time, all with severe illnesses and disabilities that gave them very short life expectancies. Eric's situation was a first for her, but she welcomed him and us with open arms, kindness, and a promise to lovingly care for him as long as we needed her to.

At this point Eric's prognosis was uncertain at best. Our trusted physician and friend, Dr. Lou Tedone, cautioned us that Eric could, as he put it, "die tomorrow or live for five to ten more years." He strongly advised us to attempt to resume a normal life. Again, we were clueless as to what that might be.

The next eight months were a roller coaster of emotions, to say the least. Jim had returned to work, thus restricting his visits to see Eric to mostly weekends. I visited him every day for the most part, often with Christian in tow, who adapted to the special environment there without question. He often played alongside the other children who couldn't interact with him, either physically or verbally. Eventually, on one of our visits, Christian walked over to me and quietly asked if his brother was going to die. I felt he already knew the answer, so I responded to him as truthfully and gently as I could in the affirmative. He solemnly nodded his head and resumed his play. My broken heart shattered just a little bit more.

That spring, we learned I was pregnant, and we were amazed at our ability to joyfully attach to this new life while sitting in the agony of watching the end of another. The next few months felt tortuous, and I often worried about the stress I was under and the possible effect it could have on my unborn child, despite reassurances from my obstetrician to the contrary.

Eric's condition deteriorated over the summer, and Dr. Tedone began gently preparing us for an end that was likely to occur soon. The morning of September 19, he phoned, stating Eric had pneumonia, a recurring issue, only this time, in his weakened condition, he felt it would be fatal. Jim and I spent the day at Eric's bedside taking turns holding him and saying our goodbyes. At 11 p.m., exhausted and six months pregnant, I agreed with those present that we should both go home to rest. Sjany promised she would sit up with Eric throughout the night until we returned.

At 5 the following morning, Dr. Tedone called to tell us our precious son had died.

Three months later, I gave birth to a beautiful baby girl, Megan Elizabeth, who was perfect in every way. She was a symbol of hope for our little family that we could somehow survive the loss of her brother and learn to live without him. We had no idea how to do it but trusted that our love for her and one another would somehow make it possible.

# CHAPTER 1

# THE LOSS

*Can this nightmare be real?*

---

Memories saturate my heart / and the
story of you spills from my eyes.
GRACE ANDREN, *SPEAKING IN TEARS*

---

The death of a child is often referred to as the "worst of all losses." As a grief counselor, I am loath to categorize it in that way, as it suggests we can quantify or qualify that level of pain. There are reasons, however, for this sentiment that are certainly valid. Child loss evokes a deep, visceral response in the average person, an incomprehension of how we would cope, and often a declaration of "I could never survive that," most often uttered by another parent.

When our children are born, we are bowled over by the rush of unconditional love we feel for them. This is usually followed by an equally large rush of fear at the enormity of this new sense of responsibility. Thankfully, the love grows and carries us. The fear is eventually relegated to the background; however, it never completely leaves, nor should it. It serves as the governor of all decisions made. This particular fear is based on our desire to protect the health and safety of our beloved offspring. The mere thought of our child's ill health is enough to strike fear in our hearts, so the concept of our child's death is completely unacceptable. It is a parent's nightmare we will never think of enduring, because we can't.

### How a Child's Death Shatters Our World

The death of a child causes the ultimate disruption of our "assumptive world," a place that is created by our values, beliefs, faith, and life experiences. It is the foundation we stand on from which we feel safe to conduct our lives, take normal risks, and develop and maintain significant relationships.

The loss of a child shatters this assumptive world, throwing the parent into a place of emotional chaos. It is as if their world has been reduced to ruins, and they stand amid the rubble for days, weeks, months, and even years. Neighbors and friends pass by, and because the loss is so unacceptable, the pain so untouchable, as long as the bereaved smiles and waves, others are happy pretending they aren't standing in utter devastation. It is not from lack of caring or desire to help; it is simply too huge for most people to comprehend.

When I think back to the accident and subsequent death of our son, one of my earliest recollections of that time is how completely startled I was by the enormity of the pain I was experiencing. How was it that a human being could sustain that level of emotional pain and not cease to exist? Would there be a point when I would? Did anyone know? I remember feeling anxious in those early days every time I used a restroom where I would see my reflection in a mirror. Surely my hair would have turned white and my face become distorted. I was always shocked that that wasn't the case but truly believed my physical appearance would eventually match my inner brokenness.

While family and friends may not have those visuals, they nevertheless feel the intensity of the grieving parent's pain and find being in their company uncomfortable. Their overwhelming desire is to try and mitigate or vanquish the sorrow for this person they love. This can sometimes lead them to say or do things that can be interpreted as insensitive or uncaring. While the bereaved parent may know the intent is to be helpful, the outcome is often a deepening of loneliness and isolation.

Over the years I have received numerous phone calls from the friends and family of bereaved parents asking me for guidance as to how they can possibly help these grieving parents. Most are immobilized by their fear of saying the wrong thing and, therefore, often end up abandoning the bereaved, afraid they will do harm. I will speak to this issue of supporting bereaved parents in a later chapter.

## A Shared Sorrow

As a grief counselor, when meeting a grieving parent for the first time, I typically disclosed my identity as a bereaved parent. It never failed to amaze me how powerful that statement was in the context of this first meeting. It always felt as if my experience was a key, unlocking a door to a sacred space of their grief. No one's loss is the same, but while I could never know how it felt to lose their child or they mine, I did know what it meant to have your child die.

There is amongst bereaved parents an instant bond, a compassion for one another—an acknowledgement of our lifetime membership in a club we did not choose to join. This connection afforded me the opportunity to work effectively and deeply with these parents. I wasn't afraid of their pain and understood its depth. I had credibility, and the trust that often takes many weeks or months to develop grew quickly.

It opened up the space for their anguish to be shared.

I encouraged parents to ask me anything based on my personal loss experience, always reserving the right to decline an answer. In twenty years, I never felt the need to say "no." Many of the questions involved topics that parents often feel reluctant to speak of with family and friends and are areas I hope to cover in the chapters ahead.

### How a Child's Age Impacts Your Grief

People frequently ask if a child's age is a significant factor in a parent's grief. The most straightforward answer is no, it doesn't matter. Whether a child is two, twenty-two, or fifty-two, the pain and perception of that loss is immeasurable. Our relationships with our children grow and evolve as they mature, so when a death occurs, we view the loss through the lens associated with the current developmental stage of that child. Having said that, I will add that, when a child is still quite young and the normal process of separation has not been completed, these deaths can feel especially gut-wrenching, as if a limb has been torn from the body. This occurs most especially for mothers or the primary caregiver.

From the moment a child is born until they leave home, there is a slow and gradual process of separation that occurs. This starts by taking short trips to the grocery store or gym, spending a few hours away while Grandma babysits, or planning a date night and leaving the kids with a babysitter. Eventually, you may enroll your kids in day-care or preschool, and after age five or six, full-time school.

At some point, there is a summer camp or maybe a vacation with a best friend's family, and all the while, as parents, we start to let go and trust our child will be safe in the world without us.

When a child dies during this time, there is often an intense physical response that can be felt as overwhelm-ingly debilitating, as if that child has literally been ripped away, coupled now with a shattering of trust. The world feels unsafe, and the illusions we had in place that allow us to venture out every day and go about our lives are seriously damaged.

## The Collapse of Our Illusions

All of us operate with a set of illusions that give us a sense of autonomy, control, and safety. If we buckle our child into an approved car seat in a car that is well maintained, we get behind the wheel and leave the house believing we will reach our destination with no incident. The reality, however, is that, while all those precautions are vitally important, we have absolutely no control over other drivers and any random catastrophes that could occur.

Obviously, it would be unhealthy to focus on unforeseen possibilities. Doing so can be paralyzing and would prevent any parent from taking normal risks and living in an emotionally healthy way. Our illusions are appropriate, constructive, and give us reasonable comfort. The death of a child destroys this armor, and it can take months or even years to repair or reassemble it.

Grief counseling can be very effective in exploring those illusions that were broken and working to build new ones that can be trusted again. Newly grieving parents often express feeling frightened and betrayed by life. If they have other children, there can be significant anxiety over their safety and well-being. The very notion of something happening to a second child is unthinkable and can grip a parent with immobilizing fear.

Well-intentioned supporters may suggest to these parents that the worst has already happened, so it won't happen again. Grieving parents feel just the opposite. The illusion that your child will outlive you has been vanquished, so what is to prevent the unthinkable from happening again?

The good news is that most bereaved parents, given time and support, find those fears do subside, and as they reconstruct their new illusions, they can tuck in behind them as a place of comfort and safety. As with most fears, especially those related to a child's death, finding a trusted counselor to process them with can be hugely helpful. Harboring those fears and holding them in silence gives them power; identifying them and talking about them typically diffuses and shrinks them to a much more manageable size.

Finding yourself in the midst of the nightmare of child loss is frightening and overwhelming, in part because we have no innate preparation for it. No parent ever imagines their child will actually die, so we have no clue what tools we may need to survive. The first step—and often the most difficult—is simply acknowledging what has happened and moving slowly into that unwanted reality. As you do, you'll begin to form the questions regarding what you may need and then begin to gather the tools that will help you answer them.

# CHAPTER 2

# THE UNTHINKABLE

*Can we survive this?*

---

Give sorrow words; the grief
that does not speak /
Whispers up the o'er fraught
heart and bids it break.
WILLIAM SHAKESPEARE, *MACBETH*

---

The unthinkable has happened. Your child has died, and for a parent faced with this grim reality, there are truly no words to describe the devastation. For children who die under the age of twenty-five, the death has most likely occurred as the result of an accident or other unexpected tragedy. For teens, this often includes suicides and drug overdoses. One of the biggest challenges you will face in those first few days or weeks is to absorb and acknowledge the death as real and permanent. Your brain accepts the "fact," but your heart is closed with resistance. The head and heart have to bump up against one another over and over again before this fact begins to etch itself into the heart's reality.

## The Importance of a Viewing

For many parents, if they were not present at the death, it may feel critically important to view their child's body, despite the condition, in order to accept and acknowledge the death. They must see with their own eyes that this unbelievable event has occurred. I recall standing in a mortuary with a mother as she stared down at her deceased eighteen-year-old who had died suddenly while away at school. She inspected every part of him, committing every feature, freckle, and line to memory. She seemed to be willing her brain to accept what she was seeing.

Quite frequently, a colleague or I would be called down to a mortuary when parents had been summoned there after the death of their child. Often our primary role was to reassure the staff that the parents' reactions were normal, albeit difficult to witness. Once there, many parents are very reluctant to leave, as it feels like abandonment. However, given time and loving support, all will do so eventually. As much as possible, mortuary staff are called upon to accommodate parents with compassion, empathy, and non-judgment. If they are not hurting themselves or anyone else, there is no harm in giving the parents the time they need with their child.

## Establishing a Gatekeeper

In the immediate aftermath of the death, there can be a deluge of phone calls and visits. From my own experience and that of the many families I have supported, appointing a gatekeeper has been very effective. This person can field calls, receive visitors (or turn them away), and organize food deliveries, flowers, etc. Every family is different, and while some of you welcome a house full of people for days on end, others will close the curtains and shut the gate, choosing to face this crisis in private. On any given day, you may do one or the other. Neither is right or wrong, and most people fall somewhere in the middle.

Universally, however, most parents are feeling shocked, numb, and immobilized. Less commonly, some may respond with hypomania (i.e., displaying inappropriate irritability, rapid speech, or frenetic energy).

---

Surrounding yourself with loving
family and friends who can
dispense emotional first aid is very
important and can be lifesaving.

---

As newly bereaved parents, you may struggle to eat
and sleep, and those normal activities can be elusive for
quite some time. It's advisable to limit your sugar, caf-
feine, and alcohol intake. Post-traumatic shock can produce symptoms of agitation, anxiety, hypervigilance, and
an overactive startle response. Most of these symptoms
do subside, but they can be frightening for the parents as
well as for those supporting them.

### Don't Be Afraid to Feel Your Feelings

A great deal of my work with newly grieving parents
involves helping to normalize their responses and allow-
ing the space to just be. Be angry, be sad, be scared, and,
in some cases, be relieved. Sometimes, you can be stuck
in a feeling for days or weeks. At other times, you may
ping-pong back and forth through a myriad of emotions
in one day or one hour. It's exhausting, and you can feel as

if you are losing your mind. There is often an overwhelming sense of "I cannot survive this." As I shared earlier in my own story, one of my first revelations regarding child loss was how shocked I was that a human being could sustain such intense emotional pain and not die from it. You won't die, but you may want to. This is a normal response, and one your family and friends will have difficulty hearing, so the tendency is not to share it.

Feeling as if you want to die from the pain of this loss is not the same as being actively suicidal. The pain you feel after your child dies can be utterly overwhelming and unrelenting. Initially it feels as if this will be a permanent state, unless you cease breathing. Any sane person would feel despair contemplating that thought and just want it to stop. This is very different from the intent to harm yourself, a condition you would definitely want to share and process with your physician, grief counselor, or other mental health professional.

It is my deeply held belief that intense sorrow needs to be witnessed by another human being. Your loss is profoundly personal, and no one can grieve for you. However, having the opportunity to periodically sit with a trusted person who is willing to share this agonizing space with you and allow you to articulate what you are feeling can be powerful and also effective in diffusing the pain. It can temporarily offset the lonely, and often very frightening, world this death has created. In the beginning, the pain is sharp and intense, but eventually, it does soften and become more of an ache. It will not always hurt as much as it does right now, a statement I repeated to my bereaved parents every visit. I'm not sure they believed me—in fact, I know most didn't—especially in those first few weeks. I totally understood but continued to stand before them as a testament to its truth.

## Gather Linking Objects

For those parents whose loss is sudden and unexpected, you may want to select a blanket or piece of clothing that has your child's scent on it and place it in a Ziploc bag. Many parents fear they will lose that scent, and while the Ziploc won't preserve it forever, it will keep it safe in those first few weeks or months. I have known parents who have derived great comfort from sleeping in their child's bed, while others find even entering the room to be too painful. Accept your own path and that of those grieving around you.

The issue of what to do with your deceased child's clothes, toys, backpacks, etc. is a sensitive question with no right or wrong answer. Every parent is different, and I encourage you to follow your heart and trust your gut.

If you are undecided, err on the side of keeping the item until you know for sure. Please do not let anyone rush you or imply that keeping your child's possessions is unhealthy or morbid. Your child's items are "linking objects," objects that give you something tangible to hold on to and help you feel closer to the child who has died. When a loss first occurs, it's impossible to wrap your mind around the mere thought of it, much less its permanence. Linking objects are invaluable in the healing process.

I clearly recall a mother I worked with whose young daughter had died suddenly in the hospital after a tragic accident. When she and her husband returned home two days later, her well-meaning friends had removed all the child's toys, high chair, etc. and put them in the garage, believing it would be less painful for her if she couldn't see them.

Nothing could have been further from the truth.

As painful as it was to come home without their daughter, the "erasing" of her presence with those tangible objects caused this mother great distress, and they were quickly moved back into the house.

Eventually, as a parent begins to reconcile the loss

and move to a place of holding the child more internally and abstractly, those objects lose their power and are released, for the most part. The one linking item I still have is my son's favorite T-shirt that says "Take a Liking to a Viking" tucked away in a dresser drawer, where I occasionally pull it out to look at and hold close. If an object feels comforting to you, keep it. Many parents I've known have taken their children's favorite shirts or articles of clothing and made beautiful quilts to have and wrap themselves in as ongoing visual reminders of their beloved children.

## Difficult Decisions Regarding Laying Your Child to Rest

One of the first major decisions a parent needs to make very quickly after a child dies is choosing a mortuary. While you are trying desperately to even grasp the idea that your precious child has died, you are asked if you want to cremate or bury the "body." Nothing is more brutal. As much as you'd like a third choice, there isn't one. Neither one will feel "right" by any means, but I suggest picking the one that feels less objectionable or painful, if that's even possible. Before any of these actions take place, you may choose to save a lock of hair or have an

imprint made of your child's hand or foot. Some mortu-
aries offer taking an imprint of a child's thumb to have
preserved in the form of a necklace or bracelet.

Another decision is where to lay your child's body to
rest, in whatever form it is in. For many parents, it is very
important to have a place to visit that is marked and clearly
shows that their child existed on this earth, however long
or short, and was loved. For those who choose cremation
and decide to scatter or bury the cremains, it is an option to
retain a small amount of ashes to keep. I have known parents who decided to put those ashes in a piece of jewelry
to wear close to their hearts or perhaps in a wind chime or
other ornament that could be placed in a memorial garden
at home. At a time of such anguish, it is difficult to make
these decisions, and hopefully you have loving family and
compassionate professionals to guide you.

---

**All the paths before you are painful,
but, whenever possible, try to
choose the least painful one.**

---

You make the best decision you can and then trust it
is what's best for you at that time.

Some parents find the cemetery site where their child is buried to be a place they are drawn to, visit regularly, and often find very difficult to leave. Others feel quite the opposite. One dad I met had to change his daily driving route so as to avoid even seeing the cemetery grounds, as it felt too painful to do so.

I visited my son's cemetery site very often in the first year or two and less so as the years progressed, and I gradually began to integrate and reconcile the loss. Many years later, I found my visits there to be much less painful, and the peace I was beginning to find in my own life was reflected in his burial spot. In fact, part of this book was written sitting in the sun next to Eric's gravestone, reflecting on his sweet and beautiful life. I marvel at how this little boy's life continues to have deep meaning and also offers me profound insight into my own.

### Accepting Help/Support from Others

The first few weeks following the death of your child are typically a blur. There's been a disruption of your "norm." Unfamiliar plates of food appear, and night and day seem indistinguishable. Numbness has mercifully taken over your body, and it can feel as if you are watching your life from a surreal vantage point. That numbness provides a critical buffer. It is not truly appreciated until after it has dissolved and the full weight of the loss begins to settle in. Now will be a very important time to create your team of support, those safe people who are able to walk all or part of this journey with you.

What makes a person safe? Someone who can listen without judgment and resists the urge to fix what you are feeling. Someone who is able to track with you on the roller coaster of your emotions with kindness, patience, and empathy.

Eric spent the last eight months of his life slowly dying in a care home twenty minutes away. My sister Jani, with her newborn in tow, accompanied me most days on the ride to and from the home. She always seemed to know whether I needed her to weep with me, make me laugh, or just sit in silence. I doubt she will ever truly know just how much her safe presence meant to me and how very helpful it was.

***

As you move forward, you must look at those people in your life who can be, and are willing and able to be, supportive of your grief journey.

***

If you are fortunate, you have many to choose from in your family and friend circles. If not, then perhaps there is a clergy member or minister to confide in, or a grief counselor you can see regularly. Another option would be attending a local support group where you can connect with other grieving parents.

When you are developing your support team of family and friends, it is important to evaluate them in terms of their desire and ability to help. Alan Wolfelt, PhD, in his book *Understanding Your Grief*, says all people in your life can be divided into thirds in regard to grief support:

> *One third of the people in your life will turn out to be truly empathetic helpers. They will be willing to be involved in your pain and suffering without feeling the need to take it away from you. They believe in your capacity to heal.*
>
> *Another third of the people in your life will turn out to be neutral in response to your grief.*
>
> *They will neither help nor hinder your grief journey.*
>
> *And the final third of people in your life will turn out to be harmful in your efforts to mourn and heal. While they are usually not setting out to intentionally harm you, they will judge you, they*

*will try to take your grief away from you, and they*
*will pull you off the path to healing.*

Obviously, you want to choose from the first group, your therapeutic third, as much as possible. They are the "lotion" people who are soft, soothing, and comforting as opposed to the "sandpaper" ones. We all have sandpaper people in our lives. Now would be the time to limit your exposure to them. Grief continually drains our emotional energy, and with it goes the sense of being able to cope. Choose to surround yourself whenever possible with those who fill you up, so you can spend the limited energy you have as you wish.

### Coping with the Changes in Your Everyday Living

When grief is at its seemingly highest level, as bereaved parents, you can feel as if you have no skin, like you are walking around with all your nerve endings exposed. It's an exquisitely painful time and therefore crucial for you to feel protected until you can move to a place of decreased vulnerability.

Grief can also make our cognitive functioning vulnerable. Normal, everyday thinking is often compromised.

Every day, our brain automatically triages what we have in front of us and sorts it into lists based on levels of importance. If you have an exam, a critical meeting, or an event to attend, it goes to the top tier of that list.

You may find, despite the other tasks at hand, your mind keeps going back to that main event. This recent loss automatically goes to the top of your triage list every day and overshadows all else. Whether you are driving, using equipment, or stepping off a curb, you are often in a daze, distracted much of the time, almost as if you were "under the influence." Many parents find these symptoms do subside over time, but until they do, it's important to just be aware of how the grief is affecting your ability to be totally present. While you are in a place of acute grief, stay with the basics.

Eat when you are hungry, sleep when you are tired, and cry as often as you need or want to. Be very gentle with your being. This is a very stressful time, so avoid additional stressors whenever you can and surround yourself with as much calm, positive energy, beauty, and love as possible.

## *Yes, You Will Survive This*

I frequently described child loss as an emotional injury and often asked the parents I was counseling to characterize how severe theirs was as if it were a physical injury. When answering that question, one dad looked me in the eye and, without hesitation, replied, "I'm in the ICU, and I'm not sure I'm going to make it." We cannot see the extent of someone's grief. Often newly bereaved parents are told, "You look great," a comment they usually find difficult to respond to. If they had walked into the room with crutches, casts, bandages, and IVs, there would be a rush to make them comfortable, and expectations would match the visibly obvious incapacity. We wouldn't ask someone with a broken leg to run a marathon, but we typically expect a grieving parent to do just that.

It's certainly not your job to educate every person you meet, but sharing this injury metaphor can be effective in helping others to better understand. More importantly, though, is that you evaluate your own injury and be kind with your expectations of yourself.

---

It will not always hurt as much as it does right now.

---

# CHAPTER 3

# ABSENCE OF JOY

*Is it possible to be happy again?*

---

Tears are not a mark of
weakness, but of power...
They are the messengers
of overwhelming grief...
and of unspeakable love.

WASHINGTON IRVING

---

In the days, weeks, and months following the death of a child, most parents are emotionally overwhelmed with the deep-seated belief that they will never again experience joy. Even merely surviving the event is uncertain. The notion of happiness or joy seems impossible and, frankly, undesirable. Imagining such a life devoid of any lightness is a contributing factor to the depression into which many parents sink. It's a heavy layer compounding those already blanketing the grieving family.

Grief is very much like a pool of water into which we are plunged, and fear will drown us. In the early stages, it will feel as if you have no control as memories, comments from others, or other unidentified triggers often push you under. Sometimes, you will find yourself hovering over the top of this pool of grief and, at other times, falling deeply and uncontrollably into the deep, dark water. As you begin to process your grief and ever so slowly reconcile the loss, your times out of the pool stretch longer, and, when you do sink in, you find you have collected the tools to assist you in climbing out. Perhaps it's a call to a trusted friend, a walk on the beach, or protected time to cry and release the emotions you have been harboring.

Over time, you may even find you choose to immerse yourself in that pool by looking at photos or sitting in your child's room. Painful as it may be to do so, your grief is also a powerful link to your child in those early stages, and your fear of it will eventually subside dramatically.

### Characteristics of Maternal Grief

Without making too many generalizations, I'd like to address some characterizations of maternal and paternal grief. As Therese A. Rando, PhD, states in her book *Parental Loss of a Child*, "Mothers may feel the physical emptiness that characterizes their inability to embrace their child. Parents may express their loss in physical terms, saying they feel 'mutilated.'"

In the weeks and months following Eric's death, I often said I felt as if he had been "ripped from me." Rando goes on to say, "The yearning, aching, and pining that accompany the separation from one's offspring are unparalleled in magnitude and urgency."

In my personal and professional experience, this period of pining and searching is the most gut-wrenching, painful, and challenging. It comes from a profoundly deep place within and is unrelenting for what seems to be an unbearable amount of time. In Rando's book, Barbara Schatz, a therapist and bereaved mother herself, states, "Mothers routinely experience intense emotional pain that is frightening and overwhelming. As one mother reported, 'I wanted to scream but was unable to utter a sound for fear of breaking some delicate thread within.'"

I personally recall feeling as if I was made of very thin glass. As I moved through my days, I worried that, at any minute, if I moved too quickly or even breathed deeply, I might shatter into a million pieces. Most of the bereaved mothers I met echoed similar sentiments.

Over the years, I worked with a few single mothers who lost their only child. During a counseling session, one such mom posed this achingly poignant question: "Am I still a mother?"

I assured her she most definitely was but had indeed lost her ability to "mother" her child. For these mothers, the bond with their only child is often particularly close, as they rely on only each other to navigate the world. This single mother directs all her love, support, and energy to her child. The space of aloneness she finds herself plunged into following this child's death can seem insurmountable. One of the many comforts couples can derive from one another is the knowledge that one other person shares the anguish. For these single mothers, it is essential to garner some support by finding a person to process their feelings with on a regular basis.

As mothers contend with the painful issue of "searching" for their child, many find it can be helpful to visually imagine where you know, believe, or hope your child to be. For many, that may be heaven or some similar version of eternity. A mother whose nine-year-old died said, every time it rained, she worried her daughter was cold and wet. Her prior faith system was currently nonexistent for her, so we worked on visualizing a "safe and warm space" to place her daughter when she felt anxious or worried about her.

Another mother, whose strong Christian faith had remained intact, visualized her teenage daughter in heaven and derived great comfort from that thought. For yet another mother, the traditional concept of heaven, as it related to her Catholicism, was unavailable as she struggled with the collapse of her connection to her church. Instead, we explored what had brought joy and peace to her nineteen-year-old son. We visualized how he might have perceived "heaven" and built a beautiful abstract space that reflected those thoughts. It gave her comfort to imagine him there, surrounded by everything he loved and valued.

There often appears to be an arbitrary timetable for grieving mothers, with twelve months being the magical number to reach. My own unrealistic expectation that I would feel "better" after a year was devastatingly unmet and subsequently made me question if, perhaps, there was something terribly wrong with me.

---

It was many years before I realized the goal was never to "get over" the loss of my child or somehow feel better. It was to learn how to reconcile it and live in a world without him.

---

It's important for parents to fully mourn and remember the life that *was*, taking as much time as needed to say goodbye. Only then can you start to reattach to the life ahead of you, a world in which your child is no longer present physically. There are many factors influencing this process, such as the age of the child, the relationship you had with them, and the level of support available to you. Seek out the people and circumstances that will aid you in this process.

## Characteristics of Paternal Grief

A father whose child has died is no less devastated by the loss than the mother is. However, he may have less access to support, both on a personal emotional level and by his family, friends, and community. Many fathers report that, in the wake of their child's death and for months after, they are asked how their wife is doing. All the concern is centered on the child's mother. Often the question "how are you doing?" is never asked of the father, which reinforces the image of a "strong macho man" in control of his emotions.

We grieve in the style of our personalities and also in the ways we have been taught. Many men are still raised to believe they shouldn't cry or express deep emotion.

Society tells them to be strong, self-sufficient, and the protectors of their families. I frequently redefined strength to the grieving dads I counseled as the willingness to courageously feel their feelings. Stoicism is not necessarily strength and is rarely helpful in the context of grief.

Many men are linear thinkers and approach grief from a problem-solving stance with the ultimate goal being to find a solution to fix the problem. When that goal cannot be achieved, many men may feel a sense of failure, and as a result, withdraw from their family. In doing so, some fathers will choose work as a respite from their grief—the longer absences from the family increasing their guilt, compounding their grief, and making it less likely they will attempt to address it. If their marriage is unstable, some fathers might find they seek out other relationships as an escape only to create additional complications of their grief. It should be noted that mothers are not excluded from this dangerous area of escapism as well.

For many, if not all, bereaved parents, there is a severe diminishment of self-esteem. It typically affects both fathers and mothers and certainly contributes to an absence of joy without much hope of its return. Viewing the world through the lens of low self-esteem makes healthy processing of intense grief much more challenging.

Most parents, regardless of the circumstances surrounding their child's death, feel they have failed in their duties as parents. I'll never forget a dinner out with my husband several years following Eric's death where he shared with me his feelings of guilt surrounding the loss. How could that be possible? He was not present at the time of the accident. He went on to say that he truly thought his love for us was so strong that it would always protect us, and so he had failed. I was so touched by this man's tenderness, and I was painfully reminded that I had no corner on guilt. Years later, in my work with grieving dads, I heard similar sentiments in painful disclosures. What I found, though, was that most parents, given time and space to process these feelings, eventually realize their intent was always to love and protect their child. Even though your child has died, it is not a failure of that intention. Sometimes it feels easier to blame yourself than to accept the cruel reality of an illness or accident.

Being "happy" again seems like a ridiculous notion, unattainable, or even unwanted. Bereaved parents know they are forever changed by the loss, and part of their grief is for the person they were before it happened. Many firmly believe the dark space they live in will be their permanent residence, and leaving it would be wrong and disloyal to their child.

### *Finding a Path toward Joy*

One of the most challenging aspects of child loss is making the decision to move away from the pain it has brought you. When your child dies, it is as if a brick wall abruptly slams down in front of you, separating you from your child. The path you were on is now blocked, and no matter how many times you throw your body into the wall, it stays immovable.

As parents, you remain at this "wailing wall," as it is your last point of contact and where you feel closest to the child who has died. The only way forward is to shift away from the wall and start down another path, but every fiber of your being tells you (especially mothers) that this is wrong and a betrayal against your child. For a parent who already feels they have failed, this perceived abandonment is not an acceptable choice. The reality, of course, is that your child who has died is not in that place of pain. They are to be found in the world that you, as a bereaved parent, must eventually reattach to. They are in the beautiful memories temporarily hidden by the heavy clouds of grief that surround the wailing wall. Having some distance from it can reveal precious everyday memories, such as a day spent at the beach, a football game you attended together, or making Sunday morning pancakes—all of them waiting to be felt, smiled at, and held close.

I would encourage every parent to stay at their wailing wall as long as they feel they need to. While there, you will periodically check to see if it is still impenetrable and if there is any possibility of reaching your child on the other side. Only when you are certain there is not, will you even consider leaving and trusting a new path is the one you must walk down. Take your time and don't be afraid to circle back a time or two.

## Combatting the Fear of Forgetting

One particular aspect of child loss that is painful—and even frightening—to parents is the thought their child will be forgotten. When you are actively grieving the loss, it is a reminder to those around you of the child who died and how important they were.

But what happens when the world (including your family and friends) appears to be moving on? When even *you* are doing the unthinkable by gradually adjusting to this new "normal"?

This thought may help:

---

When the sharpness of the pain has subsided, think about choosing a quality of your child's you can embody and emulate as a way to honor that life and its lasting significance.

---

For me, this is Eric's gentleness of spirit. Over the years, and especially in my work as a grief counselor, when a client or colleague has described my style as gentle, it is a fulfillment of that intention: a lovely reminder of how my sweet son lives on and impacts my interactions with others in a positive way.

Happiness and joy are not destinations or permanent states. We must intentionally create an environment in which happiness can occur, if only fleetingly, and memories of a life, however brief, can be treasured and shared. With courageous vulnerability, you move down the open path holding your child in your heart and embracing the joy you feel from knowing they will always be there.

CHAPTER 4

# GUILT AND SHAME

*Is forgiveness attainable?*

---

What we don't need in the
midst of struggle
is shame for being human.
BRENÉ BROWN

---

Guilt and shame are often a dominating component of the grieving process, drawing bereaved parents inward and distracting them from addressing other more pertinent issues. These twins of despair are greedy emotions absorbing the bereaved parent's limited energy and growing in proportion to their feeding our thoughts and beliefs. Unchallenged and unchecked feelings of guilt need no logic or truth to support them and can easily spiral out of control, damaging your ability to process your grief in a healthy manner. They are often veiled in secrecy, further isolating the grieving parent and deepening their diminishing self-esteem. Such a spiral can lead to a place of significant depression.

## Battling Feelings of Guilt

The death of a child has guilt intrinsically woven into its fabric. The foundation of parenthood is to protect our children and ensure they grow into, at the very least, young adulthood. If a child dies before this arbitrary time, parents feel as if they have failed, no matter the cause. If indeed the death is the result of a preventable accident or illness, the guilt levels will rise dramatically.

Child death often occurs as the result of a sudden and tragic accident or illness of some sort and may even be the outcome of actual or perceived negligence on behalf of one or both parents. As a physician once told me, "As parents, we have close calls almost daily with our children: at the beach, the park, a parking lot, or our own backyards. Ninety-nine percent of the time we shake our heads and say 'Whew, that was close' and move on with our day." For those in that 1 percent for whom the accident proves fatal for their child, it represents the ultimate failure as a parent.

This is where guilt can transform into its treacherous cousin, shame. "I *did* something wrong"—looked away, didn't go to the doctor immediately, etc.—becomes "I *am* something wrong"—a bad parent.

The feelings of guilt I experienced following Eric's accident were so profound and overwhelming that I doubted, at times, I could survive them. What can compound those feelings for many parents is the contradiction of them by loving family and friends. Faced with the towering enormity of parental grief and its threatening implications, along with an inability to know how to ease it, most supporters feel they can best support the bereaved by insisting the guilt isn't valid. The consistent message is, "You shouldn't feel this way." Unfortunately, the guilty person doesn't stop feeling guilty, but soon loses every person they have available to talk to, as their reality is denied and, with it, the opportunity to give voice to the agony they are carrying. The guilty feelings go deeper and grow larger but remain silenced and unattended.

### *The Path toward Partial Forgiveness*

Shortly after Eric's near-drowning, I spoke to a friend who is a mental health professional. When I reluctantly but desperately shared my feelings of guilt regarding the incident, he quickly said what had occurred was an "accident that could have happened to anyone." He advised me to forgive myself and move forward. I left that meeting feeling completely doomed, as I was totally unable to visualize ever accomplishing such forgiveness.

One of the most transcendent and healing moments of my grieving process came seven years after Eric's death when I met with a psychologist who was associated with our hospice program. After encouraging me to explore every aspect of my guilt and shame, he offered a concept of partial forgiveness. Because I considered 100 percent forgiveness to be unattainable, even undesirable, he urged me to consider working toward 90 or 95 percent forgiveness, retaining the remaining 5–10 percent as mine to keep. The concept of holding on to the responsibility of what happened, even if it was only 5 percent, and eventually releasing the rest, was life-altering. Holding on to 100 percent would have been soul-crushing, but releasing it all, incomprehensible. After much work, I eventually reached my goal, and the 10 percent of guilt that remains for me is exquisitely painful, to be sure, but it is manageable and occupies a very special, tender place in my heart.

One of the most stunning cases I worked on involved the death of a young girl who died violently as the result of an accident. Her father witnessed her death and held himself accountable.

When he shared with me the guilt he was feeling, it filled the room and seemed as if it could smother him. His shoulders were slumped, and he was unable to make eye contact. It was tempting to rush in and start dismantling and discounting his guilt, but instead we slowed way down, giving him ample room and encouragement to unpeel every painful layer. He was eventually able to reach the place where partial forgiveness could be introduced, although he was very reluctant to embrace the concept. A subsequent joint visit with his wife revealed why.

Despite her initial support of him, as she moved deeper into her own grief, she eased her sorrow by projecting it as anger at her husband. He offered no defense, as he felt it was deserved. Her anger, then, became a weapon she fired at him again and again, and I feared it would be fatal to him—and eventually to their marriage. To their credit, once this reality was presented to them, they worked hard to honestly address their feelings and work toward a resolution together. With her support, he was then able to continue his daunting task of reconciling the accident and shrinking his 100 percent responsibility down to a much more manageable and livable number.

## *Answering an Impossible Question*

A potential guilt-producing moment presents itself to all grieving parents at some point when they are asked by an unsuspecting person, "How many children do you have?" It could be at a soccer game, a swim lesson, or a casual encounter in a grocery line. It is a painful, heartbreaking, speechless moment with no easy answer.

To share with a complete stranger that you have lost a child, especially in the early days, feels scary and far too intimate. However, denying the precious life you are grieving feels much worse. In addition, you have no idea how this person may react if you tell them the truth, and that unknown may feel like a showstopper in itself. My advice to newly grieving parents is to, first, be prepared for the question and, second, to think ahead of how you might want to answer. For me, on any given day, it was different. If I was feeling particularly fragile or vulnerable, I just included Eric in the headcount and changed the subject. This especially applied to people I knew I was unlikely to ever see again. Other days, I may have shared the loss. The important piece to remember is that you, as a parent, control the narrative. A phrase such as, "We had three children, but our five-year-old daughter recently died. It's still too difficult to talk about. Thank you for understanding," allows you to honor your child who has died but doesn't leave the door open for discussion. Obviously, you can change the dialogue if you are feeling you want to engage in a more expanded discussion.

## *Dealing with Feelings of Guilt around Others*

Parental grief can be frightening and threatening to other parents because these bereaved parents represent a reality they know exists but relegate to "others." Without intending unkindness, many parents may utter phrases such as "I would never turn my back," or "I would have taken my child to the doctor much quicker" in order to feel protected from that "parent's worst nightmare" happening to them. Unfortunately, this response reinforces the guilt and shame the bereaved parent already feels along with the isolation and judgment from their peers. I always felt it was easier to let these statements slide, knowing they were a reflection of the speaker's fear that what happened could happen to them. If, however, the person uttering them is someone close to you, it might be wise to share with them how hurtful these sentiments feel.

Many parents report being avoided by friends, and more than one shared seeing an acquaintance turn and go the other way in the grocery store, something I experienced myself on more than one occasion. While it isn't hard to understand the discomfort of others regarding the painful event that has occurred, it is nevertheless hurtful and can be difficult to reconcile.

Often there is guilt to be found and experienced in regard to other family members or those in the extended circle. As parents, the guilt you may already be feeling can be compounded by the guilt you take on regarding other family members as you witness the effect the tragedy has on them.

Families can be compared to hanging mobiles, with each member taking up just the right amount of space to make it hang in a balanced way. When a child dies, the mobile immediately hangs crooked, and as the family members all shift around to fill in the empty space, it swings wildly back and forth, reflecting the emotional chaos the family is in. It will take quite some time before a sense of balance can be restored.

The family unit has been terribly wounded, and parents who are already devastated because they were unable to protect their child now assume guilt when they realize the pain family members are feeling, especially that of their other children. I know I'm not alone when I share how overwhelming it felt to see my husband's sorrow as well as my sweet five-year-old son's and to feel, in part, responsible for their pain. To even contemplate the grief of grandparents, aunts, uncles, and cousins was beyond my ability to absorb and yet needed to be addressed.

For friends who are asking how they can be helpful, a great task would be to do an internet search and make phone calls to find the grief support offered in the area.

---

It's vital at this point to remember each person is only responsible for their own grief and to be sure everyone in the family has access to their own support.

---

Of course, once the information is secured and suggested for the extended family, the friend's job is done. Nagging or "should-ing" will often create unintended pushback. Trusting others to walk this path in their own way offers the respect they deserve.

### Finding Empathy for Yourself

Guilt, anger, regret, and shame are all normal feelings following a loss—especially the loss of a child. These feelings can manifest in nuanced and even alarming ways, such as the unexpected relief some parents may feel after the child's death. If there was a prolonged illness or perceived suffering, feelings of relief after the death are a natural and appropriate response. You can feel relief and at the same time be utterly devastated by the loss. Parents of children who suffered years of alcohol or drug addiction can be relieved the hellish journey is over only to be buried in the guilt and anger that is so often close behind.

It's very important those feelings not be ignored or repressed, as they will grow, become more powerful, and complicate your recovery. We hold grief as energy in our bodies, and if we don't find a way to diffuse that energy, physical and emotional problems can present themselves.

Find a safe, patient, and nonjudgmental person to process your feelings with, and don't be afraid to explore every corner of your guilt. Doing so allows it to dissipate and transform itself into something much more manageable.

Most important of all, find your place of compassion for yourself.

Hear "your story" as if your best friend is telling it and try, if you can, to respond to yourself with love, kindness, and empathy.

# CHAPTER 5

# MARRIAGE

*Can we survive this as a couple?*

---

Being loved by someone
gives you strength,
while loving someone deeply
gives you courage.
LAO TZU

---

At the time of Eric's accident, Jim and I were three weeks shy of our eighth wedding anniversary. We felt strong as a couple, adored our two sons, and were devoted to spending time together as a close family unit. Money was tight, but we felt rich in knowing we had an abundance in all things that truly mattered.

I have often described the death of a child as analogous to a bomb going off in your life. You are shell-shocked and terrified as you view the devastation and feel paralyzed by the daunting task of gathering all the pieces and attempting to put them back together.

A clear memory I have of those early days is of an ICU nurse at Stanford cautioning us to take care of each other and not lose sight of our marriage. "We see double tragedies here," she said. "First the death of the child, and then the death of the parents' marriage." Jim and I were horrified, and frankly *frightened*, at the idea we could lose each other in addition to our son. That afternoon, on one of our many walks through the campus of Stanford Medical Center, we pledged to each other we would never let that happen. As hard as it was to hear, I am forever grateful to that nurse for her wise advice.

### The Importance of Effective Communication

Communication between couples is essential to a healthy partnership, and in the wake of a child's death, it is mandatory to its survival.

We were often "warned" that between 50 and 75 percent of marriages failed after a child has died. What an ominous statistic! In reality, it is nowhere near that high.

Compassionate Friends, an organization that supports bereaved parents, conducted a study that puts the post-child-death divorce rate at about 16 percent, with 4 percent of those couples stating their marriage was in trouble to begin with. That being said, it's hard to imagine anything stressing a marriage more than losing a child. If the union is strong and relatively healthy, it will be a rocky road, but most couples report feeling closer to each other as together they face the challenge before them. Subsequently, if there are cracks in the relationship, this current stress will pull them wide open, requiring time and attention to correct.

We all grieve differently, and as the grief is waning for one parent, the other, most often the mother, may find hers to be remaining constant or even increasing. Resentment can build because of this disparity. The risk of conflict rises considerably if one spouse perceives the other's grief response as an indication that parent did not love the deceased child enough. Giving each other plenty of room for differences in your individual grief response will help diffuse the situation. There is no single correct way or timeline in which to grieve, and effective, honest communication will be key to avoiding friction. Most couples find making a verbal contract with each other to be very helpful. Clearly asking for what you need (and saying what you *don't* need) from one another relieves the partner from the burden of having to guess and read minds.

## The Value of Having Your Own Support Teams

This journey of grief you are on is long and arduous, a marathon that requires patience and outside support. The following visualization is one I used often when working with bereaved couples.

Imagine you are both high up on a mountain and each of you breaks a leg. While you have both suffered the same injury, and, as such, identify and empathize with one another, neither of you is capable of getting the other down the mountain. You'll each need your own team of helpers to assist you down, all the while offering each other as much support as possible. It's essential for each to develop a team of trusted family, friends, counselors, etc. to help you down so you can focus on healing your own injury, knowing your partner is being ably assisted as well. Look for those who are capable and willing to track with you, listen with non-judgment, and allow you to process the wide range of emotions you'll be experiencing with compassion and confidentiality.

### Potential Challenges Regarding Intimacy

An area of potential discomfort for a grieving couple may be in addressing issues that arise regarding physical intimacy. For many, it is an unexpected challenge, and one they may feel uncomfortable discussing with each other or their support team. Though physical intimacy might be nearly unimaginable to some during this raw and painful time, it's an aspect of the couple's relationship that cannot be ignored. A frequent problem is the lack of interest by one or both of the bereaved parents. With the high degree of vulnerability and emotional tenderness present, it may feel comforting to one person and quite the opposite to the other. Many also state they rejected experiencing feelings of pleasure at this time of acute loss. When feeling safe to discuss these issues, most parents expressed relief in knowing their feelings were normal and often experienced by others. They welcomed the opportunity to defuse such an emotionally charged issue. For most couples, it was very comforting and reassuring to hear each other's concerns and then work toward a common goal of resuming their normal level of physical intimacy.

### *Grieving Separately but Together*

Men and women grieve differently; individuals grieve differently.

---

## When a couple loses a child, they share the loss but are going to react and respond in their own way, often in stark contrast to one another.

---

Most will find it important and helpful to give each other the room to grieve as needed.

In the first few weeks following Eric's death, my husband would stand in front of the mantle where we had a framed picture of Eric. He would stare at it for long periods of time and weep. On the other hand, I found looking at photos of him to be unbearably painful and constantly avoided viewing the various ones we had in place all over the house. In not judging one another's grief response, we avoided feeling we somehow needed to "be on the same page"—an impossible task, but one many couples believe they must strive to achieve.

I recall a family I worked with whose two-year-old son had died of cancer. There was a very large framed photograph of him hanging on the wall in the living room. It was the first thing you saw as you entered the home, the image dominating the space.

The child's father could not bear to have the photo there and insisted it be put away, despite the mother's protests that it was a comfort to her. It became an impasse they felt stuck on, unable to resolve. Eventually a compromise was reached where the photo was moved to an area of the house where viewing it was an individual choice. While, at first glance, the solution may seem easy, in the emotionally charged aftermath of a child's death, nothing is easy. An issue such as the placement of a photo can cause additional stress a couple feels unable to manage.

The death of a child causes great disruption in a family, and as mentioned earlier, is a significant stressor of the parents' relationship. Whereas, in previous stressful situations, one may turn to the other for support, these circumstances may prevent access to your primary resource (your spouse), as they need shoring up as well. Although each parent is grieving the loss of the same child, each had their own relationship with that child, and their grief will reflect those differences. The depth, length, and breadth of the mourning period is relative to the perceived importance of that relationship. It can be long and unrelenting, leaving both parents depleted on every level. One of the things Jim and I found to be helpful was to give each other permission to be wherever we needed to be in our process, never needing to apologize or explain having either a "good" or "bad" day.

### Other Stressors a Couple May Shoulder

Along with the individual grief and attention to the marriage, many parents have grave concerns for their other children who may be struggling to understand the loss of a sibling, in addition to other extended family members who may have been close to the child. Absence from work for one or both parents can mean financial stress, and just the tasks of daily living in the midst of this devastating event can be daunting and overwhelming.

With tempers short and nerves frayed, it is easy for couples to bump into one another emotionally, with unhelpful results. It's often easier to be mad than sad, and by not recognizing the underlying and ever-present grief, an explosion of emotion can occur.

Something as trivial as an unpaid bill or a child's overdue homework could be a trigger for an overreaction. Anger and defensiveness can rise and quickly take over the situation. Most couples find stopping and breathing through that wave until it subsides to be helpful in avoiding a response of hurtful comments and the inevitable damage they can cause. Prolonged and persistent sorrow is extremely fatiguing and debilitating. Couples want to remain aware of their own depleted inner resources as they interact with one another in this extraordinarily difficult time of their lives together. A grief counselor may be very helpful in offering suggestions for defusing tense situations and providing a space for you to process the many ways this loss is affecting your relationship.

## *Finding a Way to Support Your Shared Grief*

Grief is powerful and has the ability to overshadow and obstruct. While a couple's marriage may not be at the top of the list for attention, it's important to recognize when it is being neglected. Every relationship needs to be nurtured in order to thrive, and most couples find it healthy to check in with each other as a couple on a regular basis. A nightly walk around the block for even fifteen minutes can serve as valuable shared time until you can see your way to dinner and a movie or a weekend away. Only your spouse truly knows the depth of the loss and feels it to the core as well. There can be great comfort in acknowledging that fact and keeping each other close.

Just as we are changed as individuals after the death of a child, a marriage will be deeply affected and altered as well. Couples who recognize these changes and work toward accommodating and integrating them report positive results. Every night, for many months after Eric's death, I would fall into bed and begin to cry. Jim would put his arms around me, simply say, "I know," and let me cry myself to sleep, often shedding his own tears as well. It served two purposes: one, as a pressure valve releasing the day's stored grief, and two, as a reminder of our shared sorrow and unity as a couple. I was very fortunate to have a partner so compassionate, unwavering, and understanding. His love and support helped lay the foundation for my eventual healing. We celebrated our anniversary of forty-five years of marriage in 2020.

Surviving the death of our son forged a bond between us that feels unbreakable and gives us a closeness only we can understand. It is something we cherish deeply and never take for granted.

# CHAPTER 6

# FAMILY

*How will this affect our loved ones?*

---

We bereaved are not alone. We belong
to the largest company in the world—
the company of those who
have known suffering.

HELEN KELLER, *WE BEREAVED*

---

The death of a child causes enormous disruption in the family unit with immediate waves of devastation affecting siblings, grandparents, aunts, uncles, extended family, and close friends. In the first few weeks and months following Eric's death, I occasionally glimpsed the raw grief of our other family members. I recall feeling acute distress for them while simultaneously knowing I was personally incapable of offering any viable support. The reminder that other loved ones were grieving this loss was another layer on top of the seemingly insurmountable tower of pain growing larger every day.

### *How the Loss May Affect Your Parenting*

In the aftermath of a child's death, as bereaved parents struggle to absorb the loss, those with other children find their care and concern for them becomes paramount. One of the many challenges it presents emotionally is how to balance relinquishing the role of parenting the child who has died while actively parenting those who remain.

Our son Christian was five years old when Eric died, and while my grief felt debilitating, it was always offset by the motivation to get up every day and care for him as fully and lovingly as possible. Despite feeling woefully inadequate, caring for him and shortly thereafter, our newborn daughter Meggie, gave me purpose every day for which I felt very grateful. Many parents I have spoken to have relayed similar thoughts; others have expressed further anguish at their inability to rally the energy to care for their other children, thus releasing a torrent of guilt and self-recrimination.

It is a tenuous, fragile, and potentially perilous time. Remember to be gentle with your exquisitely tender heart and, whenever possible, ask for what you need. It may be time with your grief counselor, a coffee with a trusted friend, or accepting offers of childcare so you can have some time alone. It is normal to feel overwhelmed and totally unsure of your ability to continue parenting.

## *Managing the Grief of Your Other Children*

Bereaved parents are understandably very concerned regarding the grief of their other children. Many worry this loss will have a damaging effect on them for the rest of their lives. However, what I observed over many years was that *the death itself* was not necessarily the harmful event, it was what occurred *after*. In an effort to help your children grieve successfully, the following factors can help determine how your surviving children will cope:

1.  **Were parents able to "model" grief in a healthy, normal manner?**

    A parent's intense, distraught emotions are frightening for children to witness, and while normal and understandable, need to occur away from them. However, open displays of grief are understood, and tears make sense. Seeing a parent(s) cry—along with an explanation of his or her sadness—gives a child permission to do the same. Many children, aside from those who are very young, want their parents to be "OK" and will be inclined to feel it is their responsibility to take care of them.

Our son Christian shared with us he had strived to be "perfect" in the years following his brother's death, believing that doing so would minimize our sadness. Whether you are a married couple, single parent, blended family or other non-traditional family, it will be helpful and reassuring for bereaved children to know you are attending to your own grief and will help them to attend to theirs.

2. **Is the deceased child's name mentioned and memories of them shared?**

One of my clients who came in to see me in response to her husband's death shared in our first session that her sister had died when she was ten, and, following this loss, her name was never mentioned again. It felt to my client as if her sister had never existed. This woman needed to talk about and address this unresolved grief before she could tackle her current loss. Grief is patient and persistent. Avoiding it does not make it dissipate or cease to exist. Instead, it remains unresolved as it did for this woman, most of her adult life.

---

**The freedom and encouragement to talk about a sibling, tell stories, laugh, and cry, are all ways for children and their parents to grieve together and work toward reconciliation and healing as a family.**

---

3. **Are the deceased child's possessions off-limits?**

Siblings need linking objects, as do their parents. Most parents find it helpful to put away especially meaningful objects they want to preserve, and then let the children choose an item or two to keep as their own cherished memory. For very young siblings, it might be advisable to select something for them to keep as a memento for when they are older. If the children express discomfort in choosing, it would be advisable to box up clothes and possessions to be viewed and sorted at a later time. Most parents find, if undecided on whether to keep or dispose of various "things," it's prudent to err on the side of keeping. Viewing these items from a less emotional place in the future makes this task much easier, limiting the potential of future feelings of regret as well.

4. **Are there photographs available to view?**

Many parents have chosen to put together for each surviving child small photo albums of their brother or sister who has died, especially any taken of them together. Memory boxes filled with any or all of these items are wonderful ways for remaining children to honor their sibling who has died and keep as a loving reminder forever.

## How Children Grieve

Children grieve according to their developmental stage. For example, children who suffer a loss at a young age can only grieve that loss based on their developmental capability of understanding death. Consequently, they will revisit and understand the loss differently at each new developmental stage.

Christian was in kindergarten when Eric died. He used art, as many children do, to articulate his understanding of the loss. His initial drawings were of us as a family with Eric standing alongside. As the months progressed, Eric moved up and out toward the edge of the paper, eventually hovering over us at the top of the page. By first grade, Christian was not including him at all, although he mentioned him freely. Then, one day, out of the blue at age seven (his next significant developmental stage), he said, "It was my fault Eric died." He was old enough now to reprocess the loss and saw himself as the older brother in a more responsible role. Naturally I reassured him he was in no way at fault, that, as a child, he was not responsible for his brother's safety. The conversation that followed proved to be vitally important in informing me of this sweet boy's struggle with his brother's death. It was a startling reminder of the impact Eric's death would continue to have on him and our family for years to come.

Siblings who were very young at the time of the death or were born after will also grieve this loss as they come to understand its significance. Our daughter Meggie, born three months after Eric died, at age eight said one day, "I wish there was a window into heaven I could look through so I could at least see what Eric looks like in person." She expressed sadness over this brother she had never met and the role he would have played in her life. Over the years, she often wondered aloud how it would have felt to have two brothers and to be the youngest of three.

In families of two children where one dies, the remaining one is instantly an "only child," a prospect that can feel lonely, overwhelming, and undesired. A natural inclination after a loved one's death is for family members to overidealize them. This is especially prevalent for parents after the death of a child. While this is normal and harmless, within itself, it has the potential to be daunting and damaging for remaining siblings as they struggle to fill the "giant footsteps" that have been laid before them. As one young man put it to me bluntly, "No way I can compete with a dead brother. I wouldn't even try." Many surviving children have shared with me they felt "the wrong child died," interpreting their parent's grief as a diminishment of their own significance and importance. Children will naturally be protective of their parents and often feel it is their job to take care of them. Bereaved parents who are struggling to survive each day can easily and gratefully view this behavior as positive and fail to see the possible damage being done. Reassuring these remaining children that they are not responsible for taking care of their parents can aid in diffusing this situation.

While it is desperately sad and unfair for children

to face a major loss in their lives at a young age, they are remarkably resilient. If their parent or parents are open with their own feelings and foster a safe and loving space, children will process the loss in their own time and current developmental stage. If modeled in a healthy manner, this first experience of a significant death will set the tone positively for their views on loss for the rest of their lives. Like life, grief is messy and imperfect.

---

**Families will naturally struggle at times with ups and downs, but, ultimately, immense healing and the creation of an even stronger familial bond can be forged.**

---

### The Grief of Grandparents

For many families, grandparents play a vital and integral role in the family unit. Many of the issues related to parental grief pertain to grandparents as well. Their grief can be particularly acute as they lose their grandchild and, in essence, "lose" their child as well, unable to protect them from their fate as a bereaved parent. Seeing their child suffer such intense pain while knowing they cannot protect them from it can be agonizing.

When Eric died, his "Papa," Jim's father, was several years into a remission from leukemia. Eric's accident, prolonged hospitalization, and eventual passing was clearly excruciating for him, and he frequently verbalized his inability to accept the fate that had befallen his son and family. One year after Eric's death, he came out of remission and then died a year later from his cancer. While we will never know for sure, Jim and I always felt certain his broken heart led to the collapse of his health.

A grandmother I met with, whose eight-year-old granddaughter had died, described her own acute grief in painful detail. She spent an hour telling me stories of her precious granddaughter and the unique and close bond they had shared. She then articulated the deep sorrow she was experiencing at her perceived inability to help her son. She did not feel she could share her own grief with him, as she was focused solely on supporting him with his. Another set of grandparents whose four-year-old grandson died said they felt "it should have been us" instead of this young life cut short. Their anguish at this disparity was palpable.

Many grandparents are a frequent and important presence in their grandchildren's lives, offering unconditional love and support. The deep, nurturing relationship many share with these children is a bond that, when broken by death, is exquisitely painful. However, many grandparents may suffer a form of disenfranchised grief wherein their grief may be out of sight and unacknowledged. They may themselves disregard their own pain as all their care and concern will be directed toward their child, the bereaved parent.

## Advice for Extended Family Members to Support Grieving Parents

If you are a grandparent who has lost a grandchild, know that your grief is valid. You have every reason to mourn this loss fully and will need to be mindful of your own self-care. Seek out support in your community, perhaps through a local hospice. You can best help your own child by accepting and addressing your personal grief. Doing so will allow you to be more emotionally available to your family in the coming weeks and months.

Extended family members may also feel somewhat disenfranchised in regard to their grief. Friends and caring neighbors may ask about the bereaved parents but neglect to inquire about the grief of other loved ones who may be feeling the loss acutely. It's important to avoid comparing pain. Everyone's grief is their own to feel and process.

In addition, the parents will benefit greatly in being surrounded by family members who are acknowledging their own individual grief in a healthy and productive manner. When appropriate, mourn together as a family. Sometimes weeping together allows you all to move into a space where fond memories can be shared. You may have stories about their child they have never heard before and will, then, likely cherish forever. Every bereaved parent is comforted by knowing how beloved their child was by others in the family. Your willingness to sit with them in their sorrow and share this love will be an important part of their recovery and reconciliation of the loss.

## Our Children's Grief Experiences

I spoke with both my children about this chapter, asking their permission for examples of their personal experiences and any other input they may have in regard to family and sibling loss.

My son Christian wrote back in an email:

*I think it's important to keep maintaining and evaluating emotional and psychological states as we get older, even when these events are long in the past, as they shape our psyches currently and going forward.*

*I know that I carried a lot of guilt and anxiety well into my twenties and even thirties before I was able to get a handle on some of the feelings associated with that loss and the person I became because of it.*

*In many ways my life and who I am can be traced back to that event. It's through therapy and time that I have been able to look at it differently than I had previously, which was always in a negative and filtered light. There is a quote I like from one of the Harry Potter books by J. K. Rowling that talks about it in terms I really admire. Harry is worried about his connection to Voldemort and concerned that the events that happened to him have scarred him and made him a bad person or somehow spiritually broken. He tells Sirius Black (his godfather) this, and I love Sirius's response, which is: "I want you to listen to me very carefully, Harry. You're not a bad person. You're a very good person, who bad things have happened to. Besides, the world isn't split up into good people and Death Eaters (bad people). We've all got light and dark inside us. What matters is the power we choose to act on. That's who we really are."*

And my daughter Meggie wrote:

*For me, Eric's death started out as a somewhat mysterious event as a child. I knew I had a brother who had drowned, but I didn't know the specifics of his accident or that he hadn't died right away. I was an observant child and listened to a lot of adult conversations in which no one was aware of the little ears that were listening. The enigma of his accident continued for me as a kid, and I never wanted to ask much about it out of fear that I would make anyone sad. I was told a few times by extended family that I "saved my mom." While the words of my family were well-intentioned, they didn't realize the weight their words carried in my little brain. Now, as an adult, I can rationalize what they meant, but as a young child, I took that on as a full-time job. I was determined to be the "perfect" child to make up for the one my mom had lost. I also felt really gypped that I was the only one who didn't get to "meet" Eric. I thought that it was super unfair, very "baby of the family" of me. I think that's part of why I'd say things like wishing I could look into heaven, even though I don't remember saying that.*

*The memory that is tied to the biggest effect I think Eric's death had on me was around the time we put our dog Viking down. I was outside with*

*Dad, and I recall saying that I didn't understand why I couldn't give my heart to Viking and Eric so they didn't have to die. I truly wanted to give pieces of my heart to each of them so they could keep living. I really thought that if I acted "good enough," prayed super hard, or in general just tried hard enough that I could bring Eric back. This magical thinking dominated much of my childhood until I matured enough to understand that I, in fact, could not do any of that. I could not act perfectly enough to make up for my mom losing her son, and nothing I did could make me be Eric or replace him for my family.*

*This completely unrealistic idealism led to a lot of "people pleasing" and self-destructive behavior until I decided I was allowed to work through the grief that I had in regard to losing my brother. It took me a long time to acknowledge that I got to be sad too and grieve the loss of my brother, even though I was not physically present when his accident happened. After a long road of personal work with an amazing therapist, I learned how to use the caring, empathetic heart that grew out of coping with the loss of my brother. I will forever share my gratitude for life and loving nature to honor Eric.*

At the time of Eric's death, the understanding of children's grief was still in its infancy. I believe my kids, especially Christian, would have benefited greatly from insightful, compassionate intervention. At the very least, it would have been extremely helpful if I had received specific information regarding how best to support them and what to look for as potential problems. Today that information is readily available, and most bereaved parents find it to be of great value and comfort as they support their remaining children through this difficult time. Check with the bereavement coordinator at your local hospice, as they will guide you regarding literature or any programs available for your kids.

I would give anything to have spared my children the experience of personal loss so early in their lives. I know it impacted them greatly and was a factor in their growth and development.

To their credit, they have both worked hard to understand its influence, process its meaning, and accept the ways in which it shaped their lives. They are both truly extraordinary human beings who have allowed their brother's death to expand their hearts, deepen their compassion, and continue to influence them in a positive and meaningful way.

# CHAPTER 7

# SPIRITUALITY

*Is it OK to be angry with God?*

———————

When you walk to the edge
of all the light you have
and take that first step into the
darkness of the unknown,
you must believe that one of
two things will happen:

There will be something solid
for you to stand upon,
or, you will be taught how to fly.
PATRICK OVERTON, "FAITH"

———————

I was raised with a strict Catholic influence. Most of my
primary education took place while we were living in New

Zealand attending Catholic schools taught by Irish nuns and priests. As a young adult, it all felt pretty simple: go to church every Sunday, say your prayers, follow the Ten Commandments, and life will unfold the way it should. After the birth of both my sons, I fervently said my prayers every night before I fell asleep asking God to protect my boys. I had turned thirty just four days before Eric's accident and, up to that point, had not suffered a major loss or had my faith tested in any significant way. Eric's accident and subsequent death was earth-shattering and felt deeply on an emotional and physical level. On a spiritual level, it was just as devastating, and the sudden dismantling of my faith plunged me into a state of chaos amid a sea of troubled questions: *Where was God? Why hadn't he protected Eric? Were prayers useless? Where was Eric, and would I ever see him again? Did I believe in anything?*

Big questions with no answers I could trust from anyone. I felt profoundly betrayed by the God I had prayed to all my life. I directed all my anger at him and toward myself in large and equal measure.

## *Acknowledging Your Anger*

Most newly bereaved parents echo those sentiments of anger on varying levels.

We are all holistic beings, and
when we suffer a major loss, we are
affected physically, emotionally,
socially, and spiritually.

Our own particular faith system is personal and
often emotionally charged, so verbalizing our anger can
be difficult, although the anger is sometimes met with
judgment and can feel threatening to those with whom
you are sharing these thoughts. It is often the area where
euphemisms abound. "God has a plan." "Everything happens for a reason." "He's in a better place." All of which are
wholly insufficient attempts to make sense out of what
feels random and cruel.

For a grieving parent, these words often feel like
arrows that pierce the heart, as opposed to the comfort
they are intended to bring. I recall a poem I received from
a friend where the message implied how positive it was
Eric had died young because he now wouldn't suffer any
heartaches or deal with the pain associated with living a
long life. I remember feeling speechless, hurt, and anything but comforted.

Reaction to the loss of a child, on a spiritual level,

is viewed through the lens we have developed from our childhood experience and upbringing. One grieving mother whose young child died suddenly one night told me she felt God was punishing her.

She had no idea what her cardinal sin had been but knew she must have committed one, as her culture and religion reinforced this crushing thought. Armed with this belief, it was difficult for her to feel she deserved any relief from her pain and instead viewed it as reasonable and just punishment. This mother had to work very hard to challenge those beliefs and accept other ways to view this death that did not include the cruel retribution of a higher power.

## The Need to Find Answers

When a child dies, parents often rush to find a reason to explain how this devastating event occurred. Many will quickly blame themselves, no matter how erroneously, so that they "know" why it happened. Unfortunately, these thoughts can become "false facts," affecting and often complicating the grieving process. It is valuable, especially in the early stages, to find a grief counselor or other safe, trusted person to process these feelings with so as to not venture off into dangerous territory. I would define dangerous territory as a mental wilderness where our worst fears are confirmed. It is a dark and hopeless place that can foster and feed despair. It is difficult to reconcile your painful loss in such an unforgiving space.

Many parents, especially mothers, view any movement toward reconciling their loss as abandonment of their child and, therefore, not acceptable. They are often resistant to regular counseling visits or any suggestion that they resume "normal" activities of daily living. One mother I worked with strongly stated her intent in that regard.

She couldn't envision her grief diminishing in any way and stated how disloyal it felt to even have a reduction of her symptoms as a goal. During a session, around the one-year mark, she disclosed how horrified she was that, despite her desire to "stay put," she realized she was currently engaging with her other children, experiencing occasional pleasure, and attaching to life, albeit in a minimal way. Despite her resistance to doing so, she was adjusting to her circumstances. This courageous mother eventually accepted her deep, inner spirit was indeed healing despite her efforts to thwart it. She then made the decision to work toward living with more attachment and intent. She knew that doing so was not disloyal to her daughter but, instead, a loving tribute to an indomitable spirit, gone but never forgotten.

## *Examining Your Faith System*

At the time of their loss many parents may feel at odds with the particular faith system to which they are currently attached. Some religions view death as a time of celebration, believing the deceased now resides with God. For those parents who were not rejoicing at the thought of their child in heaven, many expressed hearing a message of shame. If not fully embracing the celebratory concept, the implication was that their faith was, perhaps, not as strong as it should be. Many stated they felt very stuck at this point. It appeared as if the choice was to either deny their grief, which felt impossible, or leave their church, incurring another loss they couldn't possibly absorb.

Neither is necessary.

---

A parent can, on one hand, be happy for the belief their child is in such a beautiful place of peace and happiness and, on the other hand (at the same time), be devastated at the loss they feel and grieve accordingly.

---

The feelings of happiness and grief are not mutually exclusive, and most bereaved are relieved to be reminded of this.

Over the years, I have worked with many parents who were atheist or agnostic. For them, there is no thought of "meeting again" in heaven or immersion in the love of an all-knowing God who would carry them through this devastating event. Friends and family are often at a loss to support someone who doesn't believe in God or a higher power. Because of this discomfort, they often continue to offer "it happened for a reason" comments. Some simply feel unable to offer support at all, further isolating the bereaved parents and, perhaps, inadvertently sending a message that these parents are somehow doomed because of their lack of religious faith.

To the contrary, many parents with this belief system are very focused on honoring and celebrating the life that had existed on this earth and has now ended forever. When able, they tend to look for ways to pay tribute to that life and demonstrate its value and importance through positive actions and interactions with others.

Some parents feel fortunate to find that their faith is very obvious, concrete, and accessible. It is a lifeline and solid source of comfort to naturally turn to for assurances and explanations that calm fears and promote understanding.

Parents may discover their community of faith to be supportive and nurturing with valuable resources available. Consequently, many find the faith-based counseling support offered to be very helpful and comforting. Other grieving parents find whatever faith they held to be true prior to their child's death to be greatly challenged and often altered. It's extremely important for these parents to have the freedom to take their time to restore their belief system in their own time. The anger that is frequently felt is appropriate and normal, as is the questioning of all they have known to be true. Those bereaved are encouraged to find safe places to explore these issues and to give themselves permission to take their time and sit in that place of anger, doubt, or fear for as long as they need to. Many, many times I observed parents eventually circling back to a faith system that is much deeper and more meaningful than it had been before. I know this was certainly true for me.

### Internal Changes a Parent Experiences

Any parent who has lost a child will tell you how profoundly changed they feel. In particular, mothers will share an indescribable "hole" or vacancy felt deep within. The child they gave birth to has died, subsequently causing the death of some integral part of their being as well. It can be frightening, confusing, and overwhelming. As compared with other deaths, more pronounced "loss of self" feelings occur. These can be linked to the closeness of the parent/child relationship with all the hopes, dreams, assumptions, and expectations parents have for them. The death causes a crisis of identity and diminishment of self-esteem.

Many parents share that it is this change, this loss of the person they were prior to the death, that is the most difficult to articulate to others. Family and friends just "want them back." However, the parent knows they are irrevocably altered. Some avoid social settings and gatherings where they feel pressured to show up and reassure others that they're "OK."

One of the tasks you must tackle as a grieving parent is to mourn the person you were before your child died: the person who had been unaware such sorrow and brokenness were possible; the person who didn't know this level of anguish and had been able to operate in the world without fear of encountering it. Lean into the pain, feel the loss, and take your time in mourning it. Doing so will allow you to circle back to yourself and embrace the person who emerges. Resist the urge to overexplain or justify who you are now. It is a process for everyone.

## Connecting with Your Child after Their Death

Following the death of a child, many parents are particularly vulnerable, questioning their faith, their lives, and their continued existence in them. Almost universally, parents ask one burning question: "Is my child OK? I need to know." Entering into this tender space quite often is the consideration of contacting a medium, either individually, in a group setting, or through the internet. The idea that an individual could contact your child and connect you to them, if only for a few brief moments, is an opportunity many parents are not willing to dismiss, despite any fears or skepticism they may harbor.

As a bereaved parent, I totally understand the desire to "know" my child is safe in whatever existence I hope them to be in. As a grief counselor my suggestion—if you choose to proceed into this endeavor—is to do so with eyes wide open and expectations low. You are operating without armor, at this place in time; exposed, vulnerable and desperately seeking assurances. In such a place you are at risk to be taken advantage of, further devastated, and additionally wounded.

I also encourage checking with family, friends, and medical professionals for referrals or recommendations. There are many gifted, compassionate, and professional mediums and spiritual teachers available. Their intent is to help you understand your grief and provide comfort through the connection you are seeking.

However, there are those individuals who are much less reputable and more than willing to be paid well to promise you the information you so desperately are looking for. Have on hand a counselor or trusted person willing to help you prepare beforehand and be available to process with you afterward. Take your time, research carefully, and protect your tender heart as much as possible.

The outdoors and places of beauty are particularly effective when searching for spiritual solace. A quiet garden, hike in the woods, or walk on the beach are all conducive to healing.

Alan Wolfelt, PhD, writes about "thin places" in his book *Healing the Grieving Spirit*:

> In the Celtic tradition, "thin" places are spots where the separation between the physical world and the spiritual world seem tenuous. They are places where the

CLAIRE AAGAARD

veil between Heaven and earth, between the holy and every day, are so thin that when we are near them, we intuitively sense the timeless, boundless, spiritual world. Thin places are usually outdoors, often where water and land and sky come together. You might find thin places on a riverbank, a beach, or mountaintop. Go to a thin place to pray, to walk, or to simply sit in the presence of the holy.

## Healing Your Wounded Spirit

Whether we believe in God, Buddha, the Universe, a higher power, or Mother Nature, the spiritual part of our being is wounded and challenged after the death of a child. While you may not use words like "soul" or "spirit," a deep inner part of you has been affected separate from your mind or body.

It is a time of deep personal reflection—and often agony—as you struggle with those "Big Questions" mentioned earlier.

Where is God? Where is my child? Will I see him again? What is my purpose? What do I believe? and many more…

As a grief counselor, I certainly didn't ever pretend to know the answers to these questions. I did observe great value, though, in creating a safe space for parents to ask

86

them. Often, they would struggle mightily with the process. It was in that struggle where many found the answers or even peace with *not* knowing…an acceptance of the mystery surrounding it all.

Initially, I found the very thought of exploring my own wounded spirit to be frightening and avoided doing so for quite some time. Eventually I found the courage to go to a "thin place," sit quietly, and let myself fall into the deep recesses of my truth. Slowly and over time, seeds of compassion for myself were sown and, with them, the knowledge and acceptance of grief work to be done. I knew I could not be the wife or mother my husband and children deserved without addressing the grief that had me by the throat.

If you find your spirit is troubled, keep in mind that many others have walked this uncertain path with similar questions and doubts. Many people express anger toward God and are often frightened by such unfamiliar feelings. This crisis of faith is normal within the context of such a devastating loss.

---

You are not alone, and where you are now is unlikely the place you will be tomorrow, next month, or next year.

---

Find your "thin places" and visit them regularly. With this death of your child, a deep, inner part of you has been dramatically affected. Whether you refer to it as your soul, your truth, or your inner voice, it is your wisdom—the well from which you draw your strength in troubled times. This loss you have experienced will guide you to a closer examination of life and death and prompt you to explore and redefine your views regarding meaning and purpose in your life. Lean into the pain. Go deeper. Often the frantic search for answers lies within, waiting for you to sit still and hear them.

# CHAPTER 8

# FIRSTS

*How do we cope with birthdays or holidays?*

---

Given the choice between pain and nothing, I would choose pain.
WILLIAM FAULKNER, *THE WILD PALMS*

---

Eric died in September, and a month later it was Halloween, a holiday I had never thought much of and had no real attachment to. I planned to take five-year-old Christian trick-or-treating along with my neighbor who had a son the same age. As we started down the road, it hit me like a ton of bricks. A year ago, only two weeks before Eric's accident, I had taken the boys out trick-or-treating, pushing Eric (in his tiger costume) down the same street in a stroller. Here we were, one year later, and he was gone. The first Halloween without him, and I never saw it coming. I remember being grateful for the darkness of the night and the chattiness of my neighbor as I struggled to maintain some level of composure.

Following the death of a child, parents face a barrage of "firsts." Some are obvious and often fearfully anticipated, such as the first birthday, Thanksgiving, or Christmas, while others jump up and hit us from behind. They are a little like landmines dotting your daily landscape, hidden from view until you unfortunately step on them, similar to the Halloween I described.

It could be the first time you are asked how many children you have, or the first time you sign a greeting card without including your deceased child's name. The first football season, family vacation, county fair, or Easter egg hunt—the list goes on and on. After the death of her young son, one mom found she could not bring herself to make an appointment for their annual family photograph. The thought of not including him seemed impossible to fathom, as if it would somehow put the whole surreal experience into documented reality.

As difficult and potentially debilitating as those "firsts" are, they are an integral part of our process of reconciliation as we work toward the integration and absorption of the loss. I often think back to my initial career, that of an X-ray technician working for orthopedic surgeons. Patients with a fractured bone would come in periodically for films. While still in pain and unable to bear weight on a broken leg, we could show them their X-rays and allow them to see, definitively, the bone's process of healing. In addition, we could then gauge how long their recovery would be and when full healing might take place. Unfortunately, grief does not translate in that way. We cannot view the healing of a wounded heart and spirit in a concrete way, nor can we offer a time frame for the full absorption, adjustment, and reconciliation of this life-altering event. "How long?" so many parents would ask. It was the one question often repeated, for which I dearly wished I could give a practical answer.

## Reframing the "Firsts"

I do think we can reframe these "firsts" as something more positive and possibly see them as guideposts, as we wander through the wilderness of new grief.

Making our way through them, processing what did and didn't work is helpful in preparing for those same events as they roll around again the next year and the year after that.

After refusing to make several appointments for the annual family photograph, the mother I mentioned earlier finally decided to take the portrait. She and her family gathered on the beach. They drew a large heart in the sand, wrote her son's name in the middle, and took the picture next to it.

A beautiful and courageous adjustment to their circumstances.

## First Holiday Season

For those "firsts" we can anticipate, there are some things to think about and do that will hopefully ease your way through and diffuse some of the impact. The biggest and most difficult first for most people is Christmas. Part of why the holiday season is so challenging is just that. It's a season, starting with Thanksgiving and running through the end of December, usually at least six weeks. Beyond the official time is the reminder it is coming, usually around September or even as early as August, when we are pummeled with commercials, ads, and merchandise displayed in Costco, Target, Walmart, and seemingly everywhere else. To a bereaved person, it can feel like a personal attack, evoking anxiety and fear as you wonder how you can possibly cope with it all.

The holidays are intended to be a time of great joy, family togetherness, gift giving, and thankfulness. Instead, if your child has died, the holidays can evoke extreme sadness, loneliness, and emptiness. The inability to "fit" the expectations of the seasons offers another layer of isolation.

As a bereaved parent, the last thing you may feel like doing is putting up a tree or decorating the house. However, if you have other children (especially if they are young), you will likely feel torn about negating an experience they may be looking forward to.

Most parents find it helpful to talk about the upcoming holiday as a family. If they are old enough to understand, ask your children how they feel, and look for ways to compromise. Perhaps just pick one or two things to do this first year and keep the stress and expectations low. It's helpful to acknowledge things are not "normal" and, whenever possible, give permission for each family member to feel whatever they are feeling.

Many bereaved parents find that acknowledging the child who has died is helpful as they navigate the holidays. Look for a memorial tree lighting or similar service offered in your community.

---

**Taking the time to remember your child in a special way and expressing your grief can often clear a space to move into the holiday season knowing they have been honored and are not forgotten.**

---

The hospice I worked for offered a tree-lighting ceremony, reading of names, and a video called "Faces of Love" composed of photos sent in by loved ones remembering those who had died.

Every year I was part of a team that lovingly and reverently read those precious names and viewed the beautiful faces of those no longer with us. It was sad, to be sure. It was also, however, a lovely tribute and reminder that those we have loved and lost are never forgotten.

For many years, I purchased a special candle I silently designated as Eric's. I lit it every night during the holiday season as a way to honor and remember him, inviting his spirit to be a part of our holidays. Some families choose to make a toast at Christmas or Thanksgiving dinner. Others select a child in need through the Salvation Army or similar organizations and donate a gift in their child's name.

It will be helpful to take charge where you can. So often we feel swept up in the holiday spirit, and well-meaning friends, and even family, may inadvertently make you feel guilty for not fully embracing this "joyful" time. Do the best you can, communicate your needs and feelings, be gentle with yourself, and practice good self-care.

A painful first I recall in regard to our first holiday season was opening a box of Christmas decorations and finding myself looking at Eric's stocking. Christmas boxes that haven't been opened since your child died may contain stockings, handmade decorations, and other items related to your child and past celebrations. If you want to hang your child's stocking, do so. Some families write notes and place them in it throughout the season. Preparing yourself to see them can somewhat minimize the shock.

"Firsts" are often realized by triggers we are unaware of until they happen. The holiday season is unmercifully full of them. Music, sights, sounds, and smells associated with this time of year can bombard you and overwhelm the senses. Whatever coping skills you have gathered or are currently employing will be helpful to use at these stressful times.

Eat well, get plenty of rest, and avoid excess alcohol and sugar. Stay close to your "safe" people and avoid whenever possible those who drain your energy. It may be helpful to know that the anticipation of an upcoming special day is almost always much worse than the day itself. Simply put:

+ Make a plan and keep it very simple.
+ Find a way to honor and remember your child who has died.
+ Take charge where you can.
+ Give yourself permission to feel and express your emotions.

## First Birthday

Many parents are unsure of how they should recognize or "celebrate" the birthday of their child who has died, especially the first. There is certainly no right or wrong way, and plans can be made or changed at the last minute. Some families bake a cake, sing happy birthday, and basically have a party in their child's honor. Some may make a donation to a nonprofit in their child's name, while others find it best to hunker down and quietly let the day pass.

In my experience, both personally and professionally, I find it's important to acknowledge it as a special day and to make a plan, even if the plan is to do nothing. Those parents who chose to ignore or deny the approaching day often found that that strategy backfired and were, then, at a loss to manage and prepare for the accompanying painful emotions.

I lovingly recall my sister Jani's approach to Eric's birthday. After the first couple of birthdays had passed, she said to me, "I'm tired of putting flowers on Eric's grave for his birthday. Instead, I'll just buy a gift for Christian and Meggie. He'd like that better." It was one of the many times I was reminded that love is more powerful than grief, and love is how we survive the loss.

## First Anniversary of the Death

Facing the first anniversary of your child's death can seem nearly impossible. Most parents feel they have merely survived the first year and are often fearful of reliving the events as the one-year marker approaches. To be sure, there can be a resurgence of painful emotions and a feeling of sensitivity and vulnerability echoing from a year ago.

---

**However, it is important to remember you only have to live through your child's death one time.**

---

It is not necessary to put yourself back in those early days or the death itself and relive every moment as the only way to memorialize your child.

Often bereaved parents agonize over what to "do" to commemorate this date. Nothing seems enough as they search for a way to convey how much their child was loved and how desperately they are missed. In that context, all falls short. Most find, especially for the first year, a quiet gathering of close friends and family to be the most comforting. As with the first birthday, make a plan, as simple or elaborate as you need. Make sure you set aside time in the day to "be" with your child, honoring and celebrating the cherished life that was.

### *Moving toward Reconciliation*

Eric died in September, as the autumn season began. His accident had occurred the previous November. For many years, I would feel a cloud surrounding me before I was even aware of the actual dates. A sense of deep and sometimes dark melancholy descended for much of the fall season. Many bereaved parents report something similar.

Our bodies hold a memory of past experiences and we often "feel" the time of year long before looking at a calendar. Whatever your challenging month or season is, take note and allow for increased sensitivity and vulnerability. Make those in your inner circle aware so they can best support you.

Today I still experience a little "shadow time" as fall approaches but am able to quickly move through it and embrace the changes and beauty of the season. My memories of Eric are more vivid at this time of year, and any sadness felt is easily balanced with the gratitude I feel for the opportunity to remember and connect with the love that remains unchanged.

CHAPTER 9

# CIRCUMSTANCES

*Does how it happened*
*make a difference?*

---

Whole years of joy glide unperceived
away, while sorrow counts
the minutes as they pass.
WILLIAM HAVARD

---

Early in my career, I co-facilitated a parental loss support group. On the first night, parents introduced themselves and then gave a brief description of their loss. Each story was unique. Every tragic circumstance you could imagine was shared—accidental death, illness, suicide, and even murder. Parents listened intently to each other. After these heartrending introductions, parents expressed deep compassion toward one another and began diminishing their own loss, as if each story told was "worse" than the one before. I stopped the process for a few minutes and gently reminded the group that there was no "comparing" of losses and reminded them that pain is pain is pain is pain. I remember being so awed by the level of compassion and empathy these parents had for one another as they shared the sorrow of losing a child.

While comparison may not serve us, understanding differences almost always does. I do feel it's important to briefly describe the different layers of parental grief as they relate to the circumstances of a child's death. This is not intended to be an exhaustive list but, rather, a list of those most commonly seen in my bereavement practice.

### Accidental Deaths

The Centers for Disease Control's statistics state 5 in every 100,000 children between ages 1 and 14 die from accidents. The death rate for children ages 10–19 has soared in the past few years to 45 for every 100,000 young people, with motor vehicle accidents as the number one cause, and suicides as the second.

Accidental deaths are just that: accidents. By their

very nature, they are sudden and unexpected, and it is this fact that makes them so difficult to fathom, absorb, and accept. Most parents are aware in raising their children that, while dangers lurk everywhere, 99 percent of the time we avert those "close calls." However, if you are in that fatal 1 percent...it matters not. It's 100 percent anguish.

My son had a near-drowning accident where we essentially lost him as the child he had been. However, it took ten agonizing months for him to finally stop breathing and die. I was asked more than once if I thought it would have been better or "easier" if he had died the day of the accident. My eventual response was this: Try to imagine you are standing on the railroad tracks and a train is coming straight for you, but you can't move off. Then imagine a train coming up suddenly and silently and hitting you from behind. Which one hurts more? There is no good or correct answer.

The accidental death of a child is the train hit from behind, a devastating blow no parent sees coming or has any preparation for. As with any sudden and unexpected death, there is enormous shock and trauma. This can be overwhelming and debilitating as you struggle to move through emotions and decision-making. Complicating matters—depending on age and circumstance—may be guilt over the inability to have prevented the accident from occurring and/or intense anger toward anyone deemed responsible.

For one mother, her anger toward those she held responsible for her son's death became all-consuming. While understandable, it was unrelenting and so powerful it eventually isolated her from family and friends who felt unable to offer any comfort or support. A few years later, she shared with me that, while she felt her anger had been a useful tool in surviving the loss, as her grief dissipated, the anger sat, large and looming, untouched and waiting to be resolved.

Many parents whose children have died have channeled their anger into helping them create new laws and make positive changes to existing legislation that impacted their child's death. Mothers Against Drunk Driving (MADD) and Amber's Law are two impactful examples. For some, there is a powerful call to turn their loss into something meaningful, even sacred. Most are motivated by the desire to have other parents avoid the same fate that has befallen them. It is important, however, for these parents to make sure that they are setting aside time to attend to their grief, explore and express their anger, and process their feelings, even as they strive courageously to make the world a safer place.

## *Adult Child Death*

Having your child die whether they are a toddler, a teen, or an adult is a life-altering and devastating event. However, there are many in our culture who assume the loss is less painful if the child is an adult. As mentioned earlier, pain is pain. And, while we shouldn't attempt to quantify it, there are certainly different nuances and layers that will apply to the child's age and circumstances of the death.

When an adult child dies, the parents' grief is often discounted or diminished. Some are told they should be grateful their child lived so long, as if the assumption all along was that they wouldn't. For many parents, the relationship with their adult child had evolved into friendship, so, subsequently, the parent loses not only their child but their best friend as well. When your adult child dies, you may question your own purpose in life and feel robbed of the opportunity to be a part of that child's life in a meaningful way. Often, parents experience feelings of guilt in outliving their child and agonize over thoughts that they could have done things differently to foresee this outcome.

Disenfranchised grief can occur when the cause of death is one that others find uncomfortable, such as from drugs or alcohol. Parents may experience judgment from others with subtle or not-so-subtle messages that they may have been at fault or bad parents.

Others are often unaware of the long and tortuous journey these parents have traveled—in some cases for many years—only to have the end be the death of their beloved child. Many of these parents have put their own lives on hold in order to focus on their child and work to support recovery for them. The death leaves a huge void in day-to-day life and adds to feelings of loss and emptiness.

When an adult child who is married dies, the parents may have the spouse and their grandchildren to consider and support. The love and concern for their child's family may supersede their own grief and hamper their ability and desire to seek out the support they need. If there is a spouse remaining, there could be fears or concerns regarding that spouse eventually remarrying and the possible impact on their relationship with their grandchildren. If the parents are elderly and this was an only child who has died, the concern may be focused on who will now help care for them.

As with most losses, parents will find their pain does eventually soften, and meaning and purpose returns to their lives. Most find it is helpful to be as open as possible, talking to friends and family regarding the death and the feelings surrounding it.

---

# Seek out those who knew your child to hear their stories and share happier memories.

---

Ask for what you need, and let others help and seek out support in whatever way makes sense.

## Suicide

Any death of a child can evoke feelings of shock, fear, denial, anger, depression, and anxiety. These feelings can be especially intense after a child has died by suicide. Many parents understandably personalize the death, and some may even question why their love was not enough to have prevented it. Parents are likely to struggle with the answers amid a sea of doubt and fear. Sometimes mental illness plays a role in the death, but not always.

Some children may have displayed warning signs, while others may have hidden or disguised signs and symptoms. For many parents, their child's suicide may never be understood. According to Compassionate Friends, a self-help organization offering friendship, understanding, and hope to bereaved families that have experienced the death of a child, suicide is the third leading cause of death in the United States for those aged ten to twenty-four. It is the second leading cause among adults aged twenty-five to thirty-four.

Because of the stigma attached to suicide in our society, there may be a reluctance to share the cause of death, adding a layer of unnecessary secrecy and shame. Often family members shut down in an unspoken pact to protect one another from the painful details. Keeping that secret can increase isolation and prevent you from accessing the support you need. In addition, it can serve as a barrier to openly sharing memories of your child with family and friends, thus depriving you of those feelings of potential happiness.

Suicide most commonly evokes anger. Anger at God, your child, the school, the medical community, and possibly the whole world in general. You may be especially angry at yourself for not seeing any warning signs or saving your child from reaching a place where suicide was an option and ultimate solution. Your anger is energy, and directing it constructively will be important as you struggle to manage and assimilate your grief.

Some have found writing an angry, uncensored letter to the person with whom you are upset—and then destroying it—to be helpful.

Physical exercise, whether it be a brisk walk, chopping wood, or digging in the yard, can be effective in diffusing pent-up emotion. Talking with a trusted friend who can listen without judgment is also helpful.

In my experience, the saddest legacy of suicide is the mantle of guilt and regret parents, siblings, extended family, and friends may feel following the death. One mother I worked with whose adult son had died by suicide expressed profound feelings of guilt. As his mother, she felt certain she "should" have known how emotionally tortured he felt and foreseen the solution before he chose to end his pain. Each family member may feel in some way responsible, examining last conversations and wondering if they could have said or done anything to prevent it. The big question, "Why?" may be asked over and over again, but rarely is there a clear or definitive answer available. One mother articulated to me that her work was to forgive herself for not knowing or seeing what may have been in plain sight.

Eventually many, with time and support, come to a place of acknowledgment that their child alone made the choice to end their life, and that they as parents were powerless to prevent it.

It can be especially helpful to connect with other parents whose child has also died by suicide. Many hospices offer such specialized support groups as does Compassionate Friends. You may also want to seek out professional help for individual or family grief counseling.

The National Suicide Prevention Lifeline can be reached at 1-800-273-8255.

## Illness

Today in the United States, childhood death is thankfully rare rather than commonplace. Accidents are by far the leading cause of death in children ages five to fourteen, with cancer as the second leading cause. The positive decrease in mortality rates is little comfort, however, to a parent whose child fell ill and died soon after or to those who may have cared for a child with a terminal illness. In the visualization I shared earlier, they are the ones standing on the tracks watching the train barreling toward them, powerless to make it stop.

Guilt appears to be the single most pervasive parental response to the death of a child. It is a natural reaction when we feel we have fallen short or have not lived up to the often unrealistic expectations of what it means to be a "good parent." These feelings can be especially overwhelming when a parent is facing the death of their child due to illness or disease. What did I miss? Why didn't I bring them in for care sooner? How could this situation have been prevented? The list of questions can be endless, and in the case of sudden and catastrophic illness, there's often not much time to sort through any of it.

For those parents with terminally ill children, there are certainly difficult challenges. When I had the opportunity to be in such a home as part of a hospice team, the parents almost universally focused on maintaining hope for a miracle to happen. I always assured them I would join them in that hope, and while we waited and hoped for that miracle, we could talk about and address the issues confronting them. It gave them permission to *prepare* while still holding on to the *hope* that was sustaining them. Grief often allows us to access our ability to do two things at one time…in this case, to both *hope* and *prepare*.

For those parents whose children were in pain, there were many conflicting emotions around wanting their child to live despite the pain, and then wanting the child to die because of the perceived suffering and the desperate desire for it to end. Parents have also expressed feeling negligent for leaving a child's bedside to rest or for nourishment. I, for one, have always believed that the time of death is not wholly random. Sometimes the dying person—regardless of age—will wait until they are alone in order to spare their family members.

Often families feel tremendous anguish if they are not with their child at the time of death. I choose to see it as a tenderhearted last gift.

In the aftermath of the child's death, many parents will agonize over decisions made and question their care-giving during the illness. When rested and not in crisis, it's hard not to feel you could have tried harder, done more—anything to have produced a different outcome. I found it was helpful to remind parents of what their intent was during that very painful and challenging time. Ultimately, it was to love and care for their child with all their hearts, to make decisions based on the information they had at the time and always with their child's best interest at the forefront.

## Violent Deaths

At least twenty-six thousand children and teenagers younger than eighteen years old were killed by gunfire in the United States between 1999 and 2016, according to mortality data from the Centers for Disease Control and Prevention. Firearm injuries are the third leading cause of death among children aged one to seventeen in the

United States, based on a 2017 study published in the journal *Pediatrics*.

Losing your child through gun violence or by the hand of another is an especially traumatic loss for a parent. Dropping your child off at a supposed "safe" zone, whether it be a school, movie theatre, church, or nearby park, only to have them killed by a random act of violence is the ultimate breach of trust in life itself. Many parents find themselves questioning all their assumptions and values after this complete violation of all they have known to be true. Some may feel tremendous guilt as they blame themselves for not protecting their children, for not being able to predict the unpredictable. Some may be flooded with anger, and the subsequent feelings of revenge or retribution can be frightening to experience.

Compounding all of these difficult emotions is the presence of publicity surrounding the event, contributing to parents feeling exposed, powerless, and vulnerable. Often there is a trial to follow, which can take many months. Trials can propel these parents into an agonizing limbo, further distracting them from focusing on the important grief work in front of them. One mother shared how stressful it was to see newspaper articles and hear news reports regarding the upcoming trial of the man who had killed her son. She felt retraumatized every time and found herself retreating to a place of reclusiveness in order to cope.

In the aftermath of a traumatic death, it can be helpful for you as parents to find mental health professionals to assist you in coping with the complicated emotions and reactions you may have regarding your child's death. You may find it is necessary to acknowledge and address the associated trauma you feel before you can truly tackle the grief that follows. Often there are victim witness programs available to you through your local district attorney's office. These programs can help guide you through the legal and criminal process you may be facing as well as offer individual and family counseling. If you choose to do some individual counseling, it will be wise to select someone experienced in dealing with grief and trauma.

## Perinatal Loss (Miscarriage, Stillbirth, and Neonatal Death)

One of my first encounters with perinatal loss was through a woman who had come in to see me after the death of her husband. She found herself flooded with memories of a stillborn child some twenty years earlier. She shared how she had been heavily medicated for the birth, and when she awoke, was told her baby boy had died and was "gone."

In an effort to help and protect her, this woman's husband and father had arranged for the baby to be cremated and essentially erased all evidence of his existence. She was utterly devastated. Sadly, it was fairly standard procedure for that era—remove the deceased baby, tell Mom it must have been "for the best," and encourage her to try again. As cruel as this may sound, it was all intended to minimize a mother's grief, but as this bereaved mother demonstrated, unresolved grief will continue to roll in unannounced and remain powerfully present until it is addressed, processed, and reconciled.

A baby's death before the time of birth or shortly after birth is difficult to comprehend and accept. During pregnancy, a mother has witnessed many changes in her body, listened to a heartbeat, viewed ultrasounds, and felt large and small kicks and pokes to remind her she has "company." She and the partner have likely picked a name (after much debate), know if it's a boy or girl, perhaps wondered about hair and eye color, and have eagerly awaited the day they will meet their child. They do so with all their hopes and dreams for its future clearly imprinted in their minds. Starting down that joyful road only to have it permanently blocked is extremely difficult to absorb and integrate. Most will feel huge resistance to this harsh reality.

One young mom whose baby died shortly before he was born was very distressed to learn she could obtain a death certificate for her son but not a birth certificate. "How can they acknowledge his death but deny his birth?" She felt strongly compelled to fight for his legal existence and lobbied intensely for the hospital to change its policy.

Today, in many labor and delivery units, there is a protocol in place for those mothers whose baby dies in utero either before, during, or after birth. Many have a designated bereavement counselor or identified RN to step in and coordinate support. That support may include a dedicated private room where parents/ partners can take their time and hold their baby for as long as they wish. Photographs are taken, a lock of hair saved, and foot and handprint molds preserved. These practices acknowledge that the child was real and here. Information regarding local support for this loss is also available, as are ongoing services of remembrance parents can attend in the coming months and years, if they desire.

However, despite these evolved and positive changes in perinatal death, once the parent(s) leave the hospital, they are unlikely to continue receiving that level of support. It is a difficult loss for family and friends to understand and absorb, so, unfortunately, many respond with clichés intended to comfort, only for them to have the opposite effect, leaving many parents feeling discounted and isolated in their grief.

Those women suffering from miscarriage may find they have even less support available to them. Often the loss is minimized and even dismissed with, "It wasn't meant to be" and "It was probably for the best" comments.

Miscarriage grief is very real, however.

Its intensity may not necessarily match the length of the pregnancy but is linked to other factors, including how long it took to get pregnant and how difficult that journey was (i.e., in vitro fertilization treatments). Also impacting them is how much the baby is longed for and the couple's "story" regarding this pregnancy. The partner's grief can also be intense, and finding adequate and sustained support for the deep sense of loss may be quite challenging.

My youngest sister, Tracey, suffered two miscarriages, the second of which was at twelve weeks. She describes leaving the hospital "feeling so empty." Compounding the sadness was a sense of guilt that perhaps she may have caused it by some inadvertent action. After miscarrying, many women express similar thoughts, yet there is

CLAIRE AAGAARD

very limited support available to process these feelings. There is discomfort amongst the general public in speaking about the issue of miscarriage, so these women often suffer in silence, thus complicating their grief. It can be lonely, confusing, and isolating.

---

**It will be most helpful for those suffering perinatal loss to surround themselves with family and friends who recognize this as a real loss and who respectfully listen and support the parents as they process their feelings.**

---

Most have found it to be very valuable to attend local support groups specific to this loss and/or individual grief counseling for ongoing support.

## *Special Needs*

For some parents, the death of their child comes after several years of intensive daily care due to their child's severe disability. For those parents, most often the mother, who chose to provide the care themselves, it was likely their

*118*

full-time, twenty-four-hour job. In some instances, these children are very limited in their ability to speak, ambulate, or toilet themselves. In my career, I had the privilege to witness several of these mothers compassionately, competently, and lovingly attend to their child's every need. In doing so they formed a very special relationship with their child with an intimate knowledge and understanding of every sound and movement. The bond created in these circumstances is intense and unbreakable. These parents are fierce, unrelenting advocates in a medical system they learn all too well, for a population often ignored and frequently misunderstood.

In many instances, these children are unable to progress toward independence physically, emotionally, or socially, and because of this, their parent is often unable to separate for even short periods of time. Many of these parents may, then, deprive themselves of their own basic personal needs, such as adequate sleep, good nutrition, and exercise. Those caring for a disabled child may find friendships harder to maintain and important social activities difficult to fit in the schedule. Prolonged periods of such care can lead to more social isolation, physical debilitation, emotional exhaustion, and family problems.

After the death of a disabled child, the parents I met described profound feelings of "death of self." They shared that, because of the intensity and closeness of the relationship, they felt "as one" with their child, and when that child died, it was as if they had died as well. Many said they were unable to speak about these feelings with friends or family, as it evoked fear that the parent may be suicidal. Compounding this potential isolation are the comments commonly offered, indicating "it was for the best" and "you must be relieved," further alienating the bereaved parent to a place of painful loneliness.

What has proven to be helpful to these parents is finding a place of acceptance and nonjudgmental listening in order to facilitate the processing of emotions, devoted remembrances, and a review of their child's life. Gentle encouragement of separation from "what was" to "what now is" will take time, patience, and compassion.

## Honoring How Your Child Died

Each circumstance brings with it unique challenges to overcome, and the layers of your grief will be reflective of that. Resist the urge to compare your loss in any way. Identifying and peeling back those layers is the process of your grief work, and attempting to qualify, quantify, or compare it to any other loss is not helpful or necessary and can be a drain of your limited energy. Honor the circumstances of your child's death.

---

**Every child loss, no matter the age or circumstances, needs to be valued and remembered with respect and loving attentiveness.**

---

# CHAPTER 10

# HELPERS

*What can we do to help?*

---

A best friend is the only person
that walks into your life when
the world has walked out.
SHANNON L. ALDER

---

Over the span of my career as a grief counselor, I regularly received phone calls in the aftermath of a child's death from anxious, often frantic, family and friends: "How can I help the parents? What do I say? How will they get through this?" After answering the questions and addressing the concerns, I would typically pause and ask the caller, "And how are *you* doing?" The majority of the time, the caller, often a family member or close friend, would break down and tearfully describe the deep sorrow they were feeling. Most would finish with "I'm sorry. My sadness is nothing compared to theirs."

If you are a family member or friend who is part of the team supporting a bereaved parent or parents, your grief and sadness is indeed valid and appropriate. There is no need to quantify or qualify it. The child who died may be your grandchild, niece, or nephew. Perhaps he or she was your own child's best friend. In order to be an effective helper, it will be crucial for you to honor your grief and establish your own source of support to process your feelings. Doing so will allow you to be more effectively present for the bereaved parents. In addition, you will also be modeling healthy behavior for others regarding self-care during a time of crisis.

### *What Do I Do?*

## Show up and keep showing up.

Almost universally, we have some trepidation about entering the home of parents who have lost a child. For those we love and care about, however, it's important to take a deep breath, swallow hard, knock on their door, and offer whatever they seem to need in that moment. If you have no agenda and are paying attention, you will know if they need some space. Better that they send you away than have to reach out to you for support. A little "rejection" is a small burden to bear when you truly want to be there for someone you love.

In the aftermath of a sudden and unexpected death, it is usually helpful to establish a gatekeeper, like I mentioned earlier, for those first few days. This person can monitor calls, manage the flow of visitors, set up a "meal train," and act as a much-needed buffer as the shell-shocked parents attempt to put one foot in front of the other, acknowledge the unthinkable, and try to breathe.

For Jim and me, in the first few days after Eric's accident, we felt very isolated as we were three hours away and in the pre-cell phone age. Family made frequent, much-appreciated visits, but there were long stretches of minimal contact with our "team." How comforting it would have been to receive regular text messages of love and support.

During the ten months before Eric died, as I encountered friends, I felt profound gratitude to those who were courageous enough to ask how he was and were then willing to sit in the uncomfortable space of a dismal report on his prognosis. After his death, we were so appreciative of those who showed up with hugs and tears to share, along with trays of food and other expressions of love.

Several years ago, one of my daughter's best friends suffered the loss of her brother suddenly and unexpectedly. The following day, Meggie visited Target before stopping by the mom's house where everyone had gathered. She brought with her paper plates, napkins, toothbrushes (for unexpected overnight guests), tea, snacks, and lots of tissues (the soft kind); it was essentially a basket of love.

It's a hard concept but a simple formula: show up, be yourself, and listen. Your loving presence will be very appreciated.

Many well-intentioned helpers offer the phrase "let me know if there's anything I can do." Those who are in deep grief are usually unable to imagine what that could be. Instead, offer to grocery shop or drive the parents where they need to go. Doing so will help to restore some normalcy and routine to lives that have been upended. If there are other children (and your children may be friends of theirs), a trip to the park or movies may provide great breaks for everyone. Ask if you can mow the lawn, take out the garbage, water flowers, or rake leaves.

I recall a family whose child had died a couple of months before Christmas. The parents wanted to put up a tree but felt immobilized by their grief. A close family friend brought in a tree and decorated it with the children. She also wrapped gifts and made holiday cookies, thus relieving these parents from potentially making a decision to "cancel" Christmas and disappoint their other young children.

A personal handwritten note, somewhat of a rare commodity these days, is always appreciated. If you have a fond recollection or favorite story about the child who has died, please share it. We received dozens of cards after Eric died. I kept them all in a box stored underneath our bed. Every so often (for years) I pulled them out to read again and again. They were a lovely reminder of how much he was loved and how we were as well.

Some families may suffer financial difficulties after a child's death due to the lost wages of one or both parents, high medical insurance deductibles, funeral expenses, and a myriad of other costs. If there is a fund established, you may want to contribute to it, or if not, you may want to consider starting one yourself. Depending on circumstances, purchasing gift cards to local grocery/department stores, restaurants, or movie theatres are all good choices in your efforts to offer tangible support. One additional note: be sure to let the family know who the gift card or donation is from. We received a couple of anonymous gifts, and I found it very stressful, clearly not what the donor intended. While I understood the intent was to eliminate a "thank you," it only added to our uncomfortable feelings of life being out of control.

Another helpful to-do is to research local grief support in the area where the parents live. Make phone calls and have the names of contact people for both individual counseling and group support. Write names and numbers on a card to give to the bereaved parents. When they are ready and interested, it will be so much easier for them to call directly for the help they need.

## What Do I Say?

It is the ultimate question and concern from family and friends regarding supporting parents whose child has died. It can be very difficult to find the right words to comfort a grieving parent. Many, in their effort to say something—anything—will fall back on clichés and euphemisms that may offend, hurt, or anger those they are trying to help. A loving hug and expression of empathy ("I don't know what to say" or "I'm so sorry for the pain you must be feeling") is much preferable to searching for words to "fix" an unfixable situation.

While this may be stating the obvious, avoid saying

"I know how you feel." If you haven't experienced it yourself, there's no way to know how it feels to lose a child.

Instead, you could say, "I can't possibly know how you feel, but I care deeply and can see how much you are hurting." This is also not the time to recall a previous loss of your own. Doing so can feel to the bereaved as a diminishment of their loss. When the grief is not as fresh and the parents not so emotionally tender, there may be an appropriate time to share a similar loss in the context of what you may have found to be helpful.

Many well-intentioned people will offer words of a religious or spiritual nature such as, "Everything happens for a reason," "God has a plan," "Your child is in a better place." Try to imagine being in their shoes and how you'd feel about God after hearing those words. Be especially sensitive, know the person's faith (as well as your own), and follow their lead. Let *them* tell *you* if they think it was God's plan or it happened for a reason. Perhaps you could tell them you are holding them in your heart and, if appropriate, let them know you are praying for them, if indeed you sincerely will.

Newly grieving parents can be very sensitive to well-meaning declarations of what "good parents" they are. This may seem counterintuitive as a helper in your efforts to be comforting and supportive. Bear in mind that many bereaved parents feel, no matter the circumstances, that they have failed in their role to protect their children and often cringe when hearing themselves described as "good." I distinctly recall a dear friend of mine taking me to coffee not long after Eric's death. As I attempted to describe my feelings of guilt and failure, she responded more than once with a sincere, "But you're such a good mom." I finally looked her in the eye and told her that good moms didn't let their children drown. Very unkind of me, but a true expression of the feelings I was holding inside.

As a helper, if you are able, listen to the parent you are supporting and allow them to express those difficult emotions out loud. Be that safe person and resist the urge to fix.

Many helpers express their fear of breaking down and crying when showing up to support the bereaved. It can be very comforting to grieving parents to have someone to sit and share their sorrow, listen to their process, cry with them, and offer a hug or hold a hand when needed. Just be sure it's not about you and don't cry harder than those you are there to comfort. If your intention is to be of service, you would not want the bereaved to be consoling you.

Many parents who lose young children are told, "You can have another child." Bereaved parents will tell you how offensive this comment is—as if they could replace the child they have lost with another. It can also be a sensitive topic if indeed the parents do go on to have another child. Jim and I had always planned to have three children, but during my pregnancy, the vulnerable core of my spirit worried that others may feel we were indeed attempting to replace Eric. After our daughter's birth, three months after his death, I sensed a desire from those who loved and supported us for me to completely attach to this joyful event and move away from my grief. I found it difficult to communicate my ability to celebrate the birth of our new daughter, love her and our five-year-old son with all my heart, and be bereft all at the same time. I was looking for permission (although I didn't quite realize it at the time) to continue to mourn the loss of Eric while loving and caring for my family...to be both happy and sad throughout any given day...to *grieve* and *rejoice*.

## *Keep Showing Up*

After the funeral of a close friend's daughter, I remember standing in the parking lot of the church surrounded by several of her friends. "What can we do for her?" they asked.

I suggested they look around at the hundreds of people who had shown up that day to pay their respects and to honor the young woman who had died. I then told them that 90 percent of those present would be gone after the first month. In three months, there would likely be just a handful checking in. What to do? Show up and keep showing up. Talk with their friend about her daughter, tell stories, listen to hers, laugh and cry together. Remember birthdays and anniversaries—and not just the first ones, but year after year. These milestones bring with them both happiness and sadness; be there to share both.

I have a close friend, Debbie, who has steadfastly remembered Eric's birthday every year since his death. Like clockwork she shows up every March to bring me a bouquet of flowers. I have never needed or expected her to do so, and yet the kindness and thoughtfulness of her action always touches me deeply. If you find yourself thinking of someone's child who died, send them a text or make a phone call. As time goes on, fewer and fewer people mention their beloved child's name or offer a memory. Many times, those in the helping position would say to me they were concerned that, if they brought up the loss, it would make the parent sad. The reality is that the parent is already sad. Your willingness to talk about their child allows them to share their feelings and feel less alone in their grief.

The late Elizabeth Edwards, attorney, bestselling author, and wife of former Senator John Edwards, lost her eldest son Wade in 1996. He was sixteen years old and died in a car accident. In referencing her son's death, she wrote,

> *If you know someone who has lost a child, and you're afraid to mention them because you think you might make them sad by reminding them they died—you're not reminding them. They didn't forget they died. What you're reminding them of is that you remembered they lived, and...that is a great gift.*

## The Courage to Be Present

Being present to a parent's grief can feel overwhelming and, perhaps, even frightening in its depth and scope. We should never underestimate how difficult it is to enter into the space of another's agony and bear witness to their pain. We want to "do" something that makes a difference and often ignore our greatest gift, which is our willingness to be there, to listen, and be present to another's suffering.

After Eric's death, Jim and I were surprised by some who stepped forward and equally surprised by others who stepped back. Don't avoid grieving parents or let your fear of saying the wrong thing prevent you from showing up. If you step forward, know what a gift your presence is. Love is indeed more powerful than grief, and it will shore up and sustain the bereaved.

One of the things I often told bereaved parents I was working with was that I would *harbor hope* for them. I would harbor hope, even when they felt they had none or had difficulty believing in themselves and the future before them felt dark and bleak. You can do that for the parents you are supporting. Your hope can sustain theirs in a sacred bond of solidarity until such time they can take it and believe in it themselves. The road to reconciliation after the death of a child is a long one and is often lonely and dark.

The love and support of family and friends is akin

to providing rest stops where the parents can pause, regroup, and replenish.

----

**Show up, be their beacon of light, harbor their hope, and love them through this difficult and painful time.**

----

They will never forget your courage, kindness, and presence.

# CHAPTER 11

# LOOKING AHEAD

*Will my grief ever change?*

---

Hope is being able to see that there
is light despite all of the darkness.
DESMOND TUTU

---

In the moments following my discovery of Eric in the
pool that November morning and in the weeks and
months that followed until his death in September,
I remember reeling with the shock of how sharply my
life had suddenly turned. The future loomed in front of
me like a moonscape...grey, bleak, and devoid of life. I
couldn't fathom living through another day, much less
beginning to imagine how life would look a year, five
years, ten, or twenty years later. Not only was it impossible to visualize, attempting to do so evoked crippling

anxiety and overwhelming hopelessness. How could it ever feel differently?

Most grieving parents I worked with echoed similar sentiments, and the work we did focused primarily on day-to-day coping strategies. I cautioned parents to stay in the present, in the moment. Breathe in, breathe out...always reassuring them: "It won't always hurt as much as it does right now." Eventually time becomes measured in weeks and months, not hours and days, and while the grief is ever-present, the edges begin to soften, ever so slowly, as the loss is gradually becoming accommodated. How can that be? Most of us will resist even the *notion* that this process will occur, much less embrace it. It was a surprising truth I discovered both personally and professionally, that human beings are hard-wired, for the most part, to adjust to our circumstances—even the death of a child—and to reach a place where it has cemented itself in our day-to-day reality. Moving beyond that now becomes the challenge.

## *The Evolution of Grief*

For most parents, the first year following the death of your child is truly one of survival, as described in the previous chapters. As you move into that second and third year, so many of you may question your very ability to do so. What can distinguish parental grief from other losses is its intensity and duration. While any significant loss can produce similar feelings, the loss of your child, and the grief accompanying it, is almost always prolonged, debilitating, and exhausting.

In looking ahead to that second and third year, it will be important to use the knowledge you have gleaned so far to strategize moving forward. What was helpful—however small—in that first year or two, that comforted or calmed you? What events or holidays proved to be especially difficult? Perhaps Easter slid by uneventfully, but the Fourth of July was one of those "hit you from behind" kind of days. Knowing that ahead of time gives you the opportunity to make different plans to better diffuse the difficulty of that holiday or significant date. Now, more than ever, it will be beneficial to be aware of and access your "team." Share with these family members or friends the ways in which they can be helpful and supportive. Perhaps you can express how you are feeling and what you may be struggling with. So often, verbalizing a painful problem can be helpful in itself and often will lead to a resolution.

As all of these adjustments are made and we move

toward fully releasing ourselves from the world in which our child lived and attaching to the one in which they don't, many questions are raised: "How do I keep my child's memory alive?" "Can I speak of him/her freely?" "With whom?" As with most aspects of grief, there is no real right or wrong answer, and it falls into the category of "Are you harming yourself or anyone else?" With that parameter in mind, grant yourself some grace and move through this painfully awkward time, feeling your way as you go. I found that I knew intuitively with whom I could and could not speak freely about Eric. The topic was so sacred to me that having—and practicing—that discernment produced the result I needed: a loving and meaningful conversation about my son.

Several years after Eric's death, I noticed a change in the way I was perceiving the loss. The only way I can describe it is that it had become much more personal, and I felt great comfort in that. The memory of my son was deeply embedded within my heart, and the support that had been so vital earlier on was no longer something I felt I needed in the same way. Remembrances of him were still welcomed and treasured but were, instead, received as gifts as opposed to needs. I breathed into that change with grateful relief.

## *Keeping Your Child's Memory Alive*

Keeping a child's memory alive feels so very important to every grieving parent. We feel a need to continue to parent and love this child to help ensure—and reassure yourself—that no one ever forgets they lived. Memorial headstones, benches, trees, and scholarships are all wonderful ways to achieve this goal when the need feels so vitally important. As time progresses, those needs typically lessen, and when they do, know it's a normal part of the overall reconciliation of this enormous loss and restructuring of your life.

When this happens, it can feel quite frightening. Many parents expressed to me the fear that, as they feel themselves accommodating the loss, they may start to forget or lose precious memories. One reassuring thought is this: in the beginning, the loss and all that it encompasses is in the very forefront of our minds. We can see and think of little else. As we begin to adjust and reconcile this loss and the grief begins to gradually subside, its presence starts to slowly drift out to the periphery, although it rushes back with every grief burst and trigger that occurs. Uncomfortable as that might be, it can also be comforting in its painful familiarity as opposed to the "new normal" we find so foreign.

Over time, the memories of your
child may float to the very back
of your mind, but they are always
there, never to be forgotten.

You have only to reach back and pull them forward,
intact, waiting to be remembered and held close.

## The Presence of Triggers

In those first few years following your child's death, most
parents find that the daily grief has subsided, and you
are no longer actively and symptomatically grieving as
intensely as you had in that first year or two. There is
room to breathe, and you have moved away from the
edge of the cliff. Inevitably, though, something triggers
the loss, and suddenly you are plunged into that pool of
grief you have been hovering over—and may have even
forgotten was there. It often feels very disheartening and
discouraging, as if you are "at the beginning." You aren't.
The feelings of grief are the same, whether it's been six
months or six years. The difference is all the work you
have done and tools you have gathered to reach this

place. Now is the time to employ the coping skills that you've found to be most effective in the past, whether they include an activity to do, a place to go, or a person to call. They are the rungs of the ladder leading out of the pool…when you are ready. I would gently urge you to take your time. Our grief evolves as we do, and several years later, you may find pieces of it yet to process and integrate. I was always amazed at the aspects of my grief discovered many, many years after Eric's death. I eventually accepted that they only bubbled up to the surface when I was ready to address them and open to receive the wisdom they contained.

As your grief evolves with the passage of time, your triggers generally follow suit, diminishing in their intensity and frequency, thus softening their impact. However, as I have mentioned more than once, grief is messy and unpredictable, and reminders of the loss with its accompanying grief may pop up unexpectedly. I was always astounded at the power of those feelings, so many years later, and, quite frankly, humbled by their ability to stop me in my tracks. Sometimes it was easy to just pay attention, recognize what I was feeling, and continue forward. Other times, it required much more process and digging a little deeper into my toolbox of coping skills.

Eric was to be in the graduating class of 2000, and every year our newspaper printed the faces and names of the local kids in that class. Some years I looked at them all, and some I did not. But when it was finally June of 2000, I definitely felt relieved to not have that yearly visual reminder of his absence. In contrast, when Christian and Meggie each married (eight months apart), Eric's absence suddenly leapt up in front of us and was acutely felt in a way I certainly had not anticipated. How any of us address those moments is personal and will vary from family to family. What matters most is that they are acknowledged, and you may find, if you actually lean into those feelings of grief and painful absence, it often clears a space beyond it where memories are more vivid and you can embrace the love woven throughout them.

### Three Steps Forward, Two Steps Back

We are a product of our losses: the people we have loved and the people we have lost are an integral part of who we are and, in some cases, who we become. As parents, we are forever changed by the death of our children and what that change looks like is one of the few things over which we have some measure of control.

---

## Go slowly, be gentle and forgiving, and choose your path forward with loving intention, when you are ready.

---

"Three steps forward, two steps back" may feel like the order of the day for many months or years, but eventually significant progress is made.

In Japanese culture there is a tradition called *Kintsugi*. It is the Japanese art of putting broken pottery pieces back together. Instead of throwing the item away, you glue the pieces back together using a gold adhesive, with the finished product shimmering along all the cracks. The belief is that the object is more beautiful for having been broken. This concept is often used as a metaphor for grief and loss.

Life breaks everyone at some point in their lives and sometimes it may feel as if what has broken is irreparable. In the same way, grieving parents must first assess the damage caused by their loss and then slowly move to gather the broken pieces. Examining every piece and taking time to grieve every edge and jagged point honors the deceased. By saying goodbye to how life was with their child, the parents can contemplate what life may be without them. Then parents begin assembling the broken pieces, carefully reforming them as they apply the gold adhesive to fill in the cracks. Reconstructing lives fractured by the death of a child will take much time, and the finished product may look very different. It is, as you are, beautifully imperfect, stronger now at the cracks, with the memories of your child shimmering—the gold holding you together with an unbreakable bond of love.

# CONCLUSION

## *Unexpected Gifts*

---

When you are sorrowful,
look again in your heart,
and you shall see that in truth
you are weeping for that which
has been your delight.
KAHLIL GIBRAN, "ON JOY AND SORROW"

---

Jim and I were very much in sync with our values, both believing that time spent with our growing family was paramount. We cherished every moment with our children and didn't feel we were that couple who needed to be reminded of what was important in life, or believed what had happened was intended as some sort of lesson. Eric's accident and subsequent death stripped us of all we knew to be true, and we were transported to a foreign place where there were no familiar landmarks and we didn't speak the language. It was disorienting and frightening, and we longed to go "home," a place that no longer existed as we had known it.

It was in this place of remembrance and painful soul-searching that profound levels of insight and understanding emerged. I would gladly have sacrificed all of it to have our son back, and it took a long time to reach a place of acceptance that that would never happen. Once I opened my heart to that reality, I was able to embrace the possibility that this life-altering event could alter me in a positive way.

Here is a little of what I learned:

1.  **A heart that has been broken is also wide open.**

---

It is my belief that, when we have known deep sorrow, our hearts expand and have an even greater capacity to know and appreciate meaningful joy.

---

I also felt I had an opportunity to feel and appreciate love on an even deeper level and sought

to live my life expressing that love in all my interactions with those I cared about.

2.  **Nothing that life throws at me will ever be
    insurmountable.**

    Living through and reconciling my child's
    death is the hardest thing I'll ever do. It has a per-
    manent spot at the top of the list, and everything
    else falls somewhere below…usually far below. If
    I ever feel particularly challenged by a life event,
    I remember this fact and prioritize easily. It has
    given me a sense of strength and perspective, for-
    ever present and accessible.

3.  **We have tremendous power as human beings to
    help and heal one another.**

    One of the greatest insights I received was
    learning that, when I shared my loss with another
    grieving parent, it allowed them to fully share theirs,
    and something sacred took place. It is so important
    to reach out to one another as we stumble imper-
    fectly through this life. And kindness extended
    whenever possible is transformative for all involved.

4.  **And finally, love is indeed more powerful than
    grief.**

    Love is why we mourn, and it is how we will
    survive the loss and everything that comes after.

It feels scary and uncertain for a very long time, but I found it honestly to be the only truth I could count on and the source of all wisdom and healing.

My grief slowly evolved, and as it did and I had some distance from the loss, I came to view these insights as gifts. I have made them part of Eric's ongoing legacy. His life and its impact were so positive. I wanted my life to reflect that. Sharing this journey allows me to do so. It keeps him a close and continuing presence in my life. I wish the same discoveries for you.

My intent in writing this book was to offer understanding, comfort, connection, and, most importantly, hope. For those of you coping now with the loss of your child, I am harboring that hope for you. The wish from the bottom of my heart is that this book is a symbol of that hope and has helped in some small way. It was written from, for, and with much love.

# RESOURCES

## Books

- *Understanding Your Grief* by Alan Wolfelt, PhD
- *Healing a Parent's Grieving Heart: 100 Practical Ideas after Your Child Dies* by Alan Wolfelt, PhD
- *The Courage to Grieve* by Judy Tatelbaum
- *A Broken Heart Still Beats: After Your Child Dies* by Anne McCracken & Mary Semel
- *A Grace Disguised: How the Soul Grows Through Loss* by Jerry Sittser
- *Empty Arms: Hope and Support for Those Who Have Suffered a Miscarriage or Tubal Pregnancy* by Pam Vredevelt

## For Children

- *Lifetimes: The Beautiful Way to Explain Death to Children* by Bryan Mellonie and Robert Ingpen

+ *The Tenth Good Thing about Barney* by Judith Viorst

## *Organizations and Support Groups*

+ Compassionate Friends:
  compassionatefriends.org
+ Bereaved Parents of the USA:
  bereavedparentsusa.org
+ Parents of Murdered Children:
  pomc.com
+ American SIDS Institute:
  sids.org
+ American Childhood Cancer Organization:
  acco.org
+ American Association of Suicidology:
  suicidology.org

# ACKNOWLEDGMENTS

The writing of this book was dependent on the contributions of so many.

First and foremost, I need to recognize and thank all the parents who so graciously and courageously shared the sorrow of their loss with me. I learned so much from you, and your wisdom is present on every page.

This book has resided in my heart for many years, and I am so grateful to my sister Jani Johnson for her loving and persistent encouragement to put it in writing. Thank you, sweet sissie.

Joining her was my colleague and dear friend, Dianne Thompson, with whom I worked side by side for many years in an effort to support and companion the bereaved. Your love and support, Dianne, truly made it possible.

Upon starting this project, another treasured friend, Helen Sampson, offered to edit the manuscript for me. She did so with the utmost competence, clarity, and compassion. She understood my vulnerability, and we navigated that tender space with mutual trust and shared humor. I can't thank you enough, my friend.

As the book neared completion, I was profoundly fortunate to encounter the expertise of Melissa Froehner. She was exactly the right person at the right time to make the final edits and offer invaluable direction. I'm so grateful to you, Melissa.

When I was looking to publish, I serendipitously met book agent Karen Grencik of Red Fox Literary. She embraced the manuscript and created the opportunity for it to be published. Thank you, Karen. How fortunate I was to meet you.

My final book angel is Erin McClary, editor with Sourcebooks. She believed in the importance of this book from the start and has lovingly guided it to a place I hadn't known was possible. I'm so very grateful to you, Erin.

I am part of a large, wonderful extended family, each of you so special to me and important in my life. I deeply appreciate your unwavering support in all aspects of my life.

I am especially grateful for the blessing of my beloved children and grandchildren—Christian, Sofie, Meggie, Chris, Luca, and Betty—there are no words to express the depth of my love for you all.

To Jim, my rock and best friend. How lucky I have been to have walked this path with you. You are simply amazing, and I love you so much.

And last, but certainly not least, to my sweet Eric. Your loving spirit has infused my life, our family's, and every page of this book.

---

i carry your heart with me /
(i carry it in my heart)

E. E. CUMMINGS

---

# INDEX

# ABOUT THE AUTHOR

Claire Aagaard is a certified grief counselor and critical incident responder and educator, primarily working in the hospice field for over twenty years. She served as the Director of the Center for Grief, Education and Healing in San Luis Obispo, California. She also had a private practice offering grief counseling to those suffering traumatic loss.

Claire is passionate about health and fitness. She loves to garden and greatly values time spent with her family, most especially her two grandchildren, Luca and Betty. She resides with her husband Jim in Atascadero, California.